Schöningh

EnglischWissen

Training Zentralabitur

von Patricia Anslinger
und Gisa van Els

Sprachliche Betreuung: Elin Arbin

www.schoeningh-schulbuch.de
Schöningh Verlag, Jühenplatz 1–3, 33098 Paderborn

Druck 5 4 3 2 1 / Jahr 2014 13 12 11 10
Die letzte Zahl bezeichnet das Jahr dieses Druckes.

Umschlaggestaltung: Nora Eumann, Bielefeld; unter Verwendung von Radius Images / Getty Images (vorne), Art Vandalay / Getty Images (hinten)
Druck und Bindung: westermann druck GmbH, Braunschweig

ISBN 978-3-14-041048-9

Gezielte Vorbereitung auf das Zentralabitur

Dieses Buch soll die Möglichkeit geben, sich über den Unterricht hinaus auf das Zentralabitur vorzubereiten.

Man kann mithilfe diese Buches …

… **Grundfertigkeiten zur Analyse und Produktion von Texten wiederholen**: Ausführliche Erläuterungen und Vokabelhilfen findet man im Teil GRUNDFERTIGKEITEN.

… **Grundfertigkeiten trainieren**: Die wichtigsten der im Teil GRUNDFERTIGKEITEN beschriebenen Fertigkeiten können im Teil TRAINING in einem bestimmten thematischen Kontext geübt werden.

… **Sachinformationen zu abiturrelevanten Themen nachschlagen**: Zu Beginn der Einheiten im TRAINING wird ein Überblick über das jeweilige Thema gegeben.

… **Modelltexte nachschlagen**: Für alle im Teil TRAINING zu bearbeitenden Aufgabenstellungen gibt es im LÖSUNGSHEFT Lösungen und Modelltexte.

… **Themenwortschatz wiederholen und vertiefen**: Jede der neun Einheiten im TRAINING enthält Übungen zum jeweiligen thematischen Wortschatz.

… **Analyse- und Interpretationswortschatz wiederholen**: Im Teil GRUNDFERTIGKEITEN findet man viele useful phrases, die für das Schreiben eigener Texte hilfreich sind.

… **die eigenen Texte mithilfe von Checklisten überprüfen**: Am Ende des Buches findet sich zu jeder erläuterten Fertigkeit eine CHECKLISTE, mit deren Hilfe sich eigene Texte evaluieren lassen.

… **sich einen schnellen Überblick über die geforderten Fertigkeiten verschaffen**: Die Checklisten bieten einen kurzen Überblick über die Kriterien der jeweiligen Textsorten.

… **je nach Leistungsstand differenziert arbeiten**: Zu vielen Aufgaben gibt es zusätzliche Hilfestellungen, die in Anspruch genommen werden können, aber zur Bearbeitung der Aufgaben nicht zwingend notwendig sind.

… **eine mögliche Abiturklausur bearbeiten**: Am Ende dieses Buches finden sich zwei MÖGLICHE ABITURKLAUSUREN.

Jetzt bleibt uns nur noch, viel Power beim Training und viel Erfolg im Abitur zu wünschen.

Inhalt

Seite

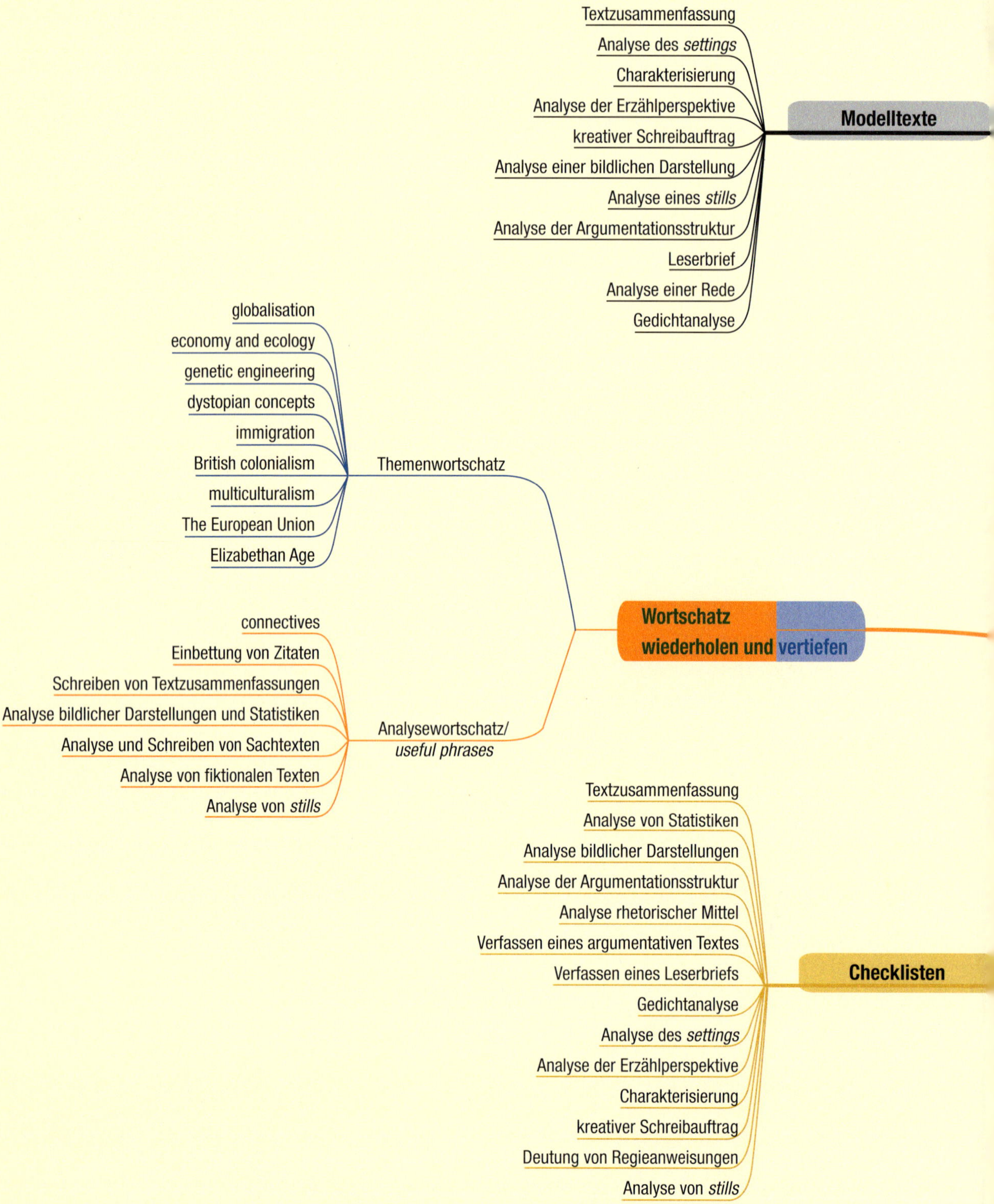
Modelltexte
Textzusammenfassung
Analyse des *settings*
Charakterisierung
Analyse der Erzählperspektive
kreativer Schreibauftrag
Analyse einer bildlichen Darstellung
Analyse eines *stills*
Analyse der Argumentationsstruktur
Leserbrief
Analyse einer Rede
Gedichtanalyse
Wortschatz wiederholen und vertiefen
Themenwortschatz
globalisation
economy and ecology
genetic engineering
dystopian concepts
immigration
British colonialism
multiculturalism
The European Union
Elizabethan Age
Analysewortschatz/ *useful phrases*
connectives
Einbettung von Zitaten
Schreiben von Textzusammenfassungen
Analyse bildlicher Darstellungen und Statistiken
Analyse und Schreiben von Sachtexten
Analyse von fiktionalen Texten
Analyse von *stills*
Checklisten
Textzusammenfassung
Analyse von Statistiken
Analyse bildlicher Darstellungen
Analyse der Argumentationsstruktur
Analyse rhetorischer Mittel
Verfassen eines argumentativen Textes
Verfassen eines Leserbriefs
Gedichtanalyse
Analyse des *settings*
Analyse der Erzählperspektive
Charakterisierung
kreativer Schreibauftrag
Deutung von Regieanweisungen
Analyse von *stills*

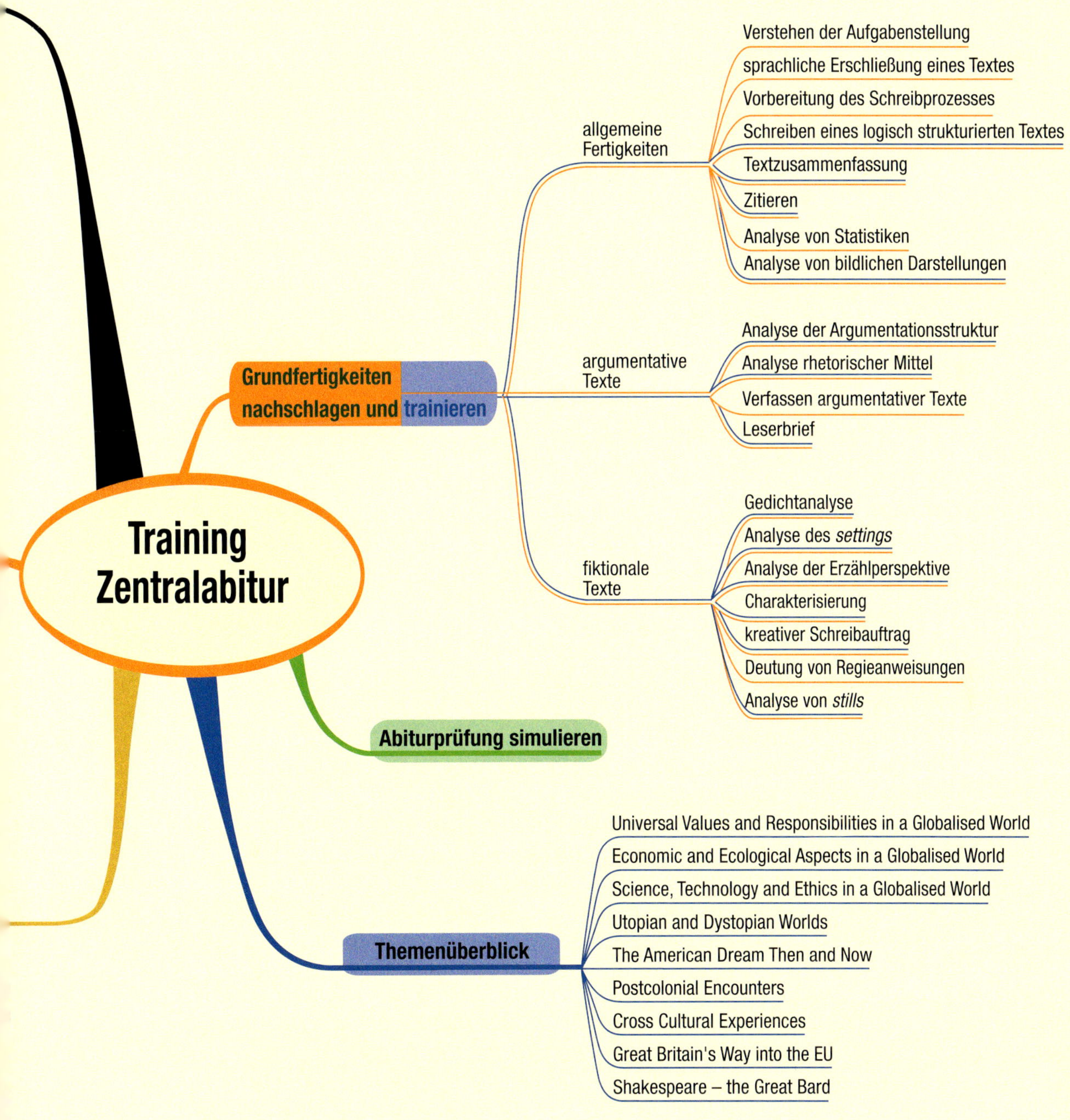

Training Zentralabitur
Grundfertigkeiten nachschlagen und trainieren
allgemeine Fertigkeiten
Verstehen der Aufgabenstellung
sprachliche Erschließung eines Textes
Vorbereitung des Schreibprozesses
Schreiben eines logisch strukturierten Textes
Textzusammenfassung
Zitieren
Analyse von Statistiken
Analyse von bildlichen Darstellungen
argumentative Texte
Analyse der Argumentationsstruktur
Analyse rhetorischer Mittel
Verfassen argumentativer Texte
Leserbrief
fiktionale Texte
Gedichtanalyse
Analyse des *settings*
Analyse der Erzählperspektive
Charakterisierung
kreativer Schreibauftrag
Deutung von Regieanweisungen
Analyse von *stills*
Abiturprüfung simulieren
Themenüberblick
Universal Values and Responsibilities in a Globalised World
Economic and Ecological Aspects in a Globalised World
Science, Technology and Ethics in a Globalised World
Utopian and Dystopian Worlds
The American Dream Then and Now
Postcolonial Encounters
Cross Cultural Experiences
Great Britain's Way into the EU
Shakespeare – the Great Bard

1. Allgemeine Fertigkeiten

1.1 Wie man Aufgabenstellungen richtig versteht

Nichts ist ärgerlicher, als bei der Rückgabe einer Klausur festzustellen, dass man offensichtlich die Fragestellung nicht oder nicht ausreichend beachtet hat. Es lohnt sich also, auf Details der Aufgabenformulierungen zu achten, da sonst ein enormer Punkteverlust drohen kann. Hierzu gehört vor allem, die Verben (**Operatoren**) zu beachten, mit denen der Arbeitsauftrag beschrieben wird.

Vorwissen über den Inhalt der *Tasks/Assignments* aktivieren

Die erste Aufgabe

- bezieht sich immer auf den **Inhalt** des vorliegenden Textes (***comprehension***).
- Es wird eine neutrale Inhalts**wiedergabe**, nicht etwa eine Interpretation oder Stellungnahme erwartet.
- Die Frage fokussiert meist auf **ausgewählte** inhaltliche Aspekte des Textes.
- Folgende Operatoren können verwendet werden: *outline, describe, state, point out, summarise.*

- Describe the situation and the different attitudes towards divorce depicted in this extract.
- Summarize what we learn about the protagonists, their dreams, their past experience and present situation.
- Point out what the speaker says about the present challenges America has to face and what he considers the only possibility to meet them.

Die zweite Aufgabe

- verlangt immer eine **Analyse** des vorliegenden Textes (***analysis***).
- Die **Machart** des fiktionalen oder nicht-fiktionalen Textes soll untersucht werden: Wie werden die Effekte erzielt, die erzielt werden sollen?
- Es wird erwartet, dass alle Erkenntnisse durch Verweise auf den Text **belegt** werden (→ S. 15 f.).
- Niemals dürfen rhetorische, stilistische oder erzählerische Mittel nur benannt werden, sondern müssen auf jeden Fall **gedeutet bzw. auf ihren Effekt hin analysiert** werden.
- Folgende Operatoren können verwendet werden: *analyse, examine, characterise, explain, illustrate, interpret, compare.*

- Analyse how the protagonist's exceptional situation is emphasised in the excerpt. Consider both content and language.
- Examine how the author tries to convince his readers that urgent action must be taken to prevent "the decline of our way of life" (l. 59). Refer to the use of language and the argumentative techniques he employs.

Die dritte Aufgabe

- verlangt entweder einen **persönlichen Kommentar** zu einer im Text aufgeworfenen Problemstellung (evaluation: *comment*) und/oder eine **produktionsorientierte** Auseinandersetzung mit dem Text (evaluation: *re-creation of text*).
- Man kann in den meisten Fällen zwischen dem Verfassen eines Kommentars oder einer produktionsorientierten Aufgabenstellung **wählen**.
- **Produktionsorientierte Aufgabenstellungen sind beispielsweise**: Verfassen eines Leserbriefs/eines formalen/informellen Briefs/einer Rede/eines Tagebucheintrags, das Schreiben eines Interviews, das Fortführen einer Erzählung
- Das Bearbeiten produktionsorientierter Aufgabenstellungen setzt voraus
  - dass man das geforderte **Textformat** beherrscht (z. B. Leserbrief, formaler Brief).
  - dass man das erforderliche **sprachliche Register** beachtet: Ein Tagebucheintrag unterscheidet sich bezüglich Wortschatz und Syntax z. B. erheblich von einem Interview mit einem Politiker.
  - dass man auf den vorliegenden Text **Bezug** nimmt und dem Inhalt des Textes **nicht widerspricht.**
- Die Aufforderung, einen persönlichen Kommentar zu verfassen, kann durch folgende Operatoren eingeleitet werden: *comment on, discuss, justify, evaluate, contrast, assess.*

- Comment on the position of women in Indian communities in Britain. Refer to problems of divorce as described in this text.
- Compare the means of control described in this article with various means of control in the society of Fahrenheit 451 and discuss which kind of control seems more threatening.
- Discuss the protagonist's dream and compare it to different versions of the American Dream you have come across in literary and/or non-literary texts.

Sorgfältiges Lesen der Tasks/Assignments

Da die Aufgabenstellungen häufig sehr komplex sind, kann es sinnvoll sein, jeweils die **wichtigsten Informationen zu markieren**, um sich aktiv zu vergegenwärtigen, was in der Aufgabenstellung verlangt wird.

- Describe the situation and the different attitudes towards divorce depicted in this extract.
- Summarize what we learn about Cándido and America, their dreams, their last experience and present situation.
- Analyse how Modern Auntie's exceptional situation is emphasised in the excerpt. Consider both content and language.
- Discuss America's dream and compare it to different versions of the American Dream you have come across in literary and/or non-literary texts.

1.2 Wie man sich vorgegebene Texte sprachlich erschließt

Die Möglichkeit, zweisprachige Wörterbücher zu benutzen, verführt zuweilen dazu, kostbare Zeit mit dem Nachschlagen von Vokabeln zu verschwenden, deren Bedeutung man sich ohne Weiteres hätte herleiten können. Um **Zeit zu sparen**, sollte man zunächst alle anderen **Methoden der Vokabelerschließung** ausschöpfen, bevor man zum Wörterbuch greift.

Bezug zu anderen Wortarten

She could no longer bear his negligence. It had to be the air of poverty surrounding her. Or was this just a mean assumption, a groundless suspicion.	neglect = vernachlässigen → Vernachlässigung poor = arm → Armut assume = annehmen → Annahme suspect = verdächtigen → Verdächtigung

Bedeutung von Vor- und Nachsilben

Vorsilbe	Bedeutung	Beispiele
un/im/in/ir/dis-	Gegenteil	uncertain, impatient, indisputable, irregular, dishonest
mis-	falsch	to misspell, to misinterpret
re-	wieder, zurück	to rewrite, to react
over-	zu viel	overweight, to overeat, to overrate
under-	zu wenig	to underestimate, understatement
sub-	unter	subheading, subconscious
super/supr[…]-	mehr als	superhuman, supertanker, supremacist
inter-	zwischen	to interact, to intervene
counter/anti-	gegen	counterproductive, antisocial
Nachsilbe	**Bedeutung**	**Beispiele**
-ful	voll von	beautiful, cheerful, powerful
-less	ohne	meaningless, powerless, emotionless, needless
-able/ible	möglich, fähig	affordable, payable, understandable, devisible

Verwandtschaft mit Wörtern anderer Sprachen

There has been vehement protest and lots of confusion. Needless to say, they have attracted much attention.	Deutsch: vehement, Protest, Konfusion, Attraktion Französisch: attention, véhément, confusion, attractif Lateinisch: vehemens, protestor, confusio, attraho

Erschließen der Bedeutung aus dem Kontext

What happens when people profess different religions and inhabit the same locality?	sinngemäß: unterschiedlichen Religionen angehören; am selben Ort wohnen

1.3 Wie man Schreibprozesse vorbereitet

Relevante Informationen farbig markieren und am Rand kennzeichnen

assonance: use of dark vowels → sad, melancholic atmosphere

hardly any verbs; static verbs → static; motionless (feeling of resignation)

A widow bird sat mourning for her love a

image of winter: cold; hard → reflection of feelings

upon a wintry bough; b

parallelism → emphasis

the frozen wind kept on above, a

the freezing stream below. b

(Percy Bysshe Shelley, 1792–1822)

Things naturally in motion are motionless.

Den Aufbau des vorgegebenen Textes visualisieren (flow chart)

Towards a Global Economy

centrally planned economy of Soviet Union collapsed (early 1990s)

neo-liberal politics:

↓

- privatisation of state-owned enterprises
- cuts in social services
- change of labour laws (more part-time jobs, more flexibility required → hiring-and-firing mentality)

← increase of efficiency and profits in a global economy

\+
- developed countries
  - outsourcing
  - merging of companies
- developing countries: emergence of new jobs

–
free trade not working for majority of the world
- power of multinationals → greater than political power
- increase in inequality
  - nationally
  - internationally

Eigene Ideen strukturieren

Zuerst pro, dann contra!

Das wichtigste Argument kommt am Schluss!

designer babies?

pro (1.)	con (2.)
no illness	unforeseeable consequences
child of your dreams	discrimination against disabled people
best genetic endowment → successful future	playing God
…	…

personal opinion: **against**; reasons:
…

Why is the speech convincing?

effect: involving listeners

rhetorical devices:
- rhetorical questions (e. g. l. 2; l. 5; ll. 3–6)
- use of first person plural (e. g. l. 9; l. 10)

effect: appealing to the listeners' emotions

rhetorical devices:
- drastic and vivid examples (e. g. ll. 1–3)
- …

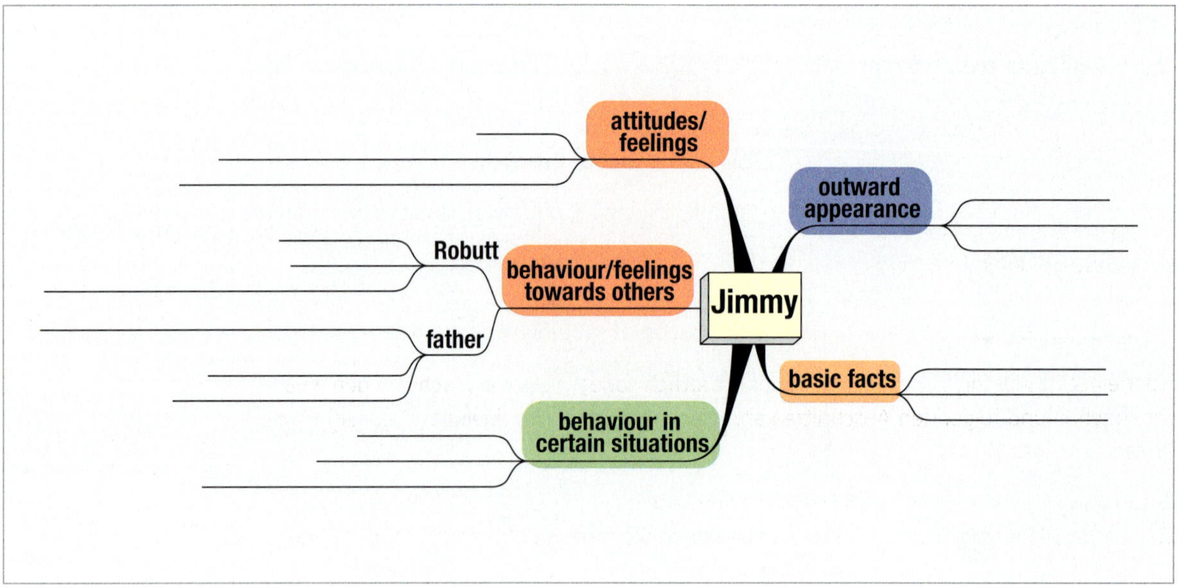

1.4 Wie man logisch strukturierte Texte schreibt

Struktur des Gesamttextes

In der Regel besteht jeder gute Text aus **drei Teilen**:

Einleitung *(introduction)*

In manchen Fällen muss in der Einleitung der **Text genannt werden, auf den Bezug genommen wird**.

- The given text is an excerpt from the short story *Indian Camp* by E. Hemingway. (→ Zusammenfassung, S. 16 f.)
- Your article *Violence in early childhood* (April 6th) has touched me. (→ Leserbrief, S. 27)

In anderen Fällen wird das **Thema** genannt:

- Many people think that smoking shouldn't be allowed in public places … (→ argumentativer Text, S. 25 f.)
- The speaker uses many rhetorical devices to convince his audience of his opinion that … (→ Analyse einer Rede, S. 22 f.)

Hauptteil (*body/main part*)

- Handlung/Hauptthesen (→ Zusammenfassung, S. 16 f.)
- Argumente (→ argumentativer Text, S. 25 f.)
- Analyse rhetorischer Mittel (→ Analyse einer Rede, S. 22 f.)

Zusammenfassung/Schlussfolgerung (*conclusion*)

- All in all, I think that there are lots of convincing arguments against smoking in public places. (→ argumentativer Text, S. 25 f.)
- In general, the speaker tries to convince his audience by appealing to their conscience. (→ Analyse einer Rede, S. 22 f.)

Struktur der einzelnen Abschnitte

Jeder einzelne Abschnitt, der sich nicht nur **inhaltlich** sondern auch **optisch** von den vorangegangenen und folgenden Abschnitten absetzen muss, ist in sich wiederum schlüssig konstruiert.

1. topic sentence	(These/Inhalt des Abschnitts in Kurzform)
2. body of the paragraph	(Die These des Abschnitts wird durch Fakten, Beispiele und andere Details näher erläutert)

[…] Another aspect to consider is that pre-implantation diagnostics normally results in destroying all the embryos not wanted by the couple. (***topic sentence***) What if the doctor finds out that only one of the three embryos created by in-vitro-fertilisation does not have the mother's hereditary disease? Of course, only this one will be implanted into the mother's womb whereas the other two will be destroyed – or should one say killed? These embryos will just be regarded as having flaws and therefore as being of no use whatsoever, regardless of the fact that they are human beings. (***body of the paragraph***) […]

Logische Verknüpfung der einzelnen Sätze und Abschnitte

Die Gedankengänge in den verschiedenen Textteilen müssen nachvollziehbar verknüpft und damit logisch strukturiert werden. Hierbei helfen *connectives*, die in keinem Text fehlen dürfen.

Improve your text – Use connectives!	
To show order	**Um zu strukturieren**
To begin with …	Zunächst …
Firstly (secondly, thirdly, etc.) …	Erstens, zweitens, …
Next …	Als nächstes …
Finally …	Abschließend …
To express your opinion	**Um die eigene Meinung auszudrücken**
From my point of view …	
In my opinion …	Meiner Meinung nach …
The way I see it …	
To my mind …	
Personally, I am convinced that …	Ich bin persönlich überzeugt, dass …
To compare and contrast things	**Um Dinge zu vergleichen und zu kontrastieren**
Although …	Obwohl …
Compared to … this is …	Verglichen mit … ist dies …
On the one hand … on the other hand …	Einerseits … andererseits
To express an opposite point of view	**Um eine gegenteilige Meinung auszudrücken**
But in my opinion …	Aber meiner Meinung nach …
Despite this/in spite of the fact … I think	Obwohl … denke ich …
I, however, …	Ich jedoch …
In contrast to …	Im Unterschied zu …
Instead of (+ -ing form) …	Statt …
All the same, I believe …	Dennoch glaube ich …
To refer to something or someone	**Um sich auf etw./jem. zu beziehen**
According to …	Gemäß …
Considering …	Wenn man … bedenkt …
To express or add ideas	**Um Ideen auszudrücken oder zu ergänzen**
Additionally …	Darüberhinaus …
Moreover …	Außerdem …
Furthermore …	
Admittedly …/I have to admit that …	Ich muss zugeben, dass …
To express reason and purpose	**Um den Grund und Zweck auszudrücken**
As …	Da …
Because of this …	Wegen der/des …; Deswegen
Consequently …	In Folge dessen …
In order to …	Um zu …

To express reason and purpose	Um den Grund und Zweck auszudrücken
Thus ...	Deswegen ...
That explains why ...	Das erklärt warum ...
That is why ...	
Therefore ...	Daher ...
For this reason ...	
To express condition	**Um Bedingungen auszudrücken**
Even if ...	Sogar wenn ...
If ...	Wenn/Falls ...
Provided that ...	Wenn sichergestellt ist, dass ...
To show consequences and conclusion	**Um Folgen und Schlussfolgerungen aufzuzeigen**
All in all ...	Zusammenfassend ...
In conclusion one might say that ...	Zusammenfassend kann man sagen, dass ...
Consequently ...	Daher ...
It follows that ...	Daraus folgt dass ...

1.5 Wie man Erkenntnisse am Text belegt

Bei jeder Textanalyse – sei es die Analyse eines literarischen oder eines Sachtextes – müssen **Erkenntnisse am Text belegt werden**, damit der Leser/die Leserin die Gedankengänge nachvollziehen kann.

Möglichkeiten, auf den Text zu verweisen

- direktes Zitieren

> The author stresses that "America will turn its wealth to the rest of the world and help end poverty" (l. 2 f.).

- Paraphrasieren

> The author is of the opinion that the whole world will benefit from America's wealth (cf. l. 2 f.).

- Einbettung des Zitates in den Satzzusammenhang

> Whereas the author emphasises that the USA "will turn its wealth to the rest of the world" (l. 2) I strongly believe that ...
> Although the author argues that "America will [...] help end poverty" (l. 2 f.) he does not accept that ...
> Will the Americans really "turn [their] wealth to the rest of the world" (l. 2)?

Zitationsregeln

- Zitate müssen **wörtlich** aus dem Text übernommen werden. Der Satz mit dem **eingebauten Zitat** muss **grammatikalisch korrekt** sein:
  - Auslassungen werden mit [...] markiert.
  - Grammatikalisch nötige Ergänzungen/Veränderungen des Zitats werden ebenfalls in eckige Klammern gesetzt.
- Seiten und Zeilen werden folgendermaßen angegeben:
  - p. 6, l. 7
  - p. 6, l. 7 f. (Zeile 7 und die darauf folgende Zeile)
  - p. 6, ll. 7 ff. (Zeile 7 und die darauf folgenden Zeilen)
  - pp. 6–7
  - p. 7, ll. 1–8
  - p. 7, l. 6–p. 8, l. 4

Improve your text – Useful phrases

To give an example, on page 5 in line 3 it ...
This passage (ll. 8–25) reveals the author's intention.
Another example of ... is to be found in line 2, where ...
This example/sentence/chapter shows that/illustrates that/suggests that/explains why ...

1.6 Wie man Texte zusammenfasst

53 f. | 86 | 4 f.; 14

- Describe the situation and the different attitudes towards war depicted in this extract.
- Point out what the author says about the American Dream.

Die erste Aufgabe in einer Oberstufen – und Abiturklausur bezieht sich immer auf den Inhalt des Textes (→ S. 8). Je nach Operator und Aufgabenstellung muss der Inhalt des gesamten Textes wiedergeben oder nur Teile des Textes zusammengefasst werden.

Die Textzusammenfassung bildet immer die **Grundlage** für die in der zweiten Teilaufgabe verlangte Analyse und muss daher alle relevanten Informationen enthalten.

Folgende Schritte können zur Vorbereitung und zum Schreiben der Zusammenfassung hilfreich sein:

1. Sorgfältiges Lesen der **Aufgabenstellung** – Was genau ist verlangt?
2. Unterstreichen relevanter Informationen mit **Bleistift**
3. Unterstreichen von Schlüsselwörtern mit Textmarker und Zusatzinformationen mit Rotstift
4. **Visualisierung des Textaufbaus** – entweder am Rand des Textes oder auf Konzeptpapier (→ S. 11)

5. Schreiben der Zusammenfassung
   - **einleitender Satz** (Text, Autor, Publikationsjahr)
   - **Simple Present** (Grundtempus)
   - **eigene** Worte
   - Zusammenhänge zwischen den einzelnen Aspekten durch **logische Verknüpfungen** der Sätze deutlich machen (→ S. 14 f.)
   - **keine Textverweise**

Improve your text – Useful phrases

The extract from the short story … by … is about/deals with … It is set in … in the year …
The given text is an extract from a speech given/delivered by … in the year …
The article … by … published in *The Guardian* on *12th October 2010* is about …
It can be divided into three parts: Firstly … Secondly … Finally …

1.7 Wie man Statistiken analysiert und interpretiert

☑ 87

- Analyse how the given graph proves the development claimed in the editorial.
- Analyse whether the line graph can be regarded as proof for the claims made in the editorial.

Ergebnisse von statistischen Erhebungen und Umfragen werden in der Regel der Übersichtlichkeit wegen graphisch dargestellt. Man unterscheidet im Wesentlichen vier verschiedenen Arten der graphischen Darstellung:

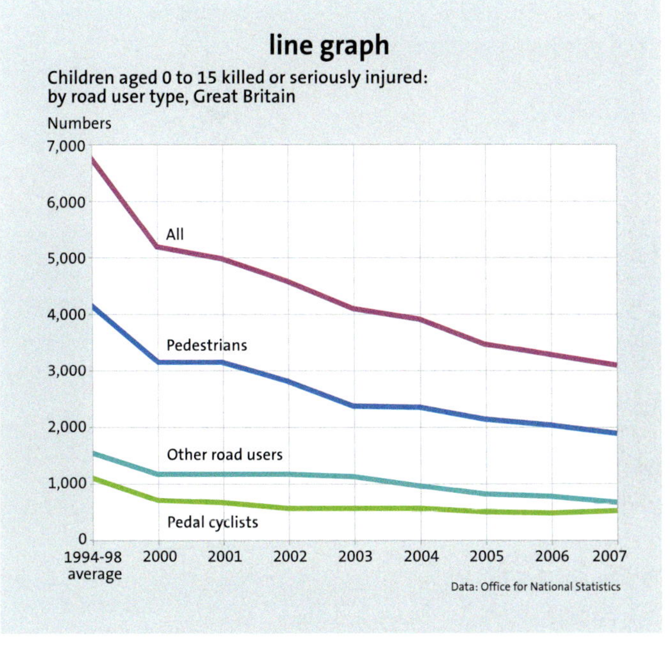

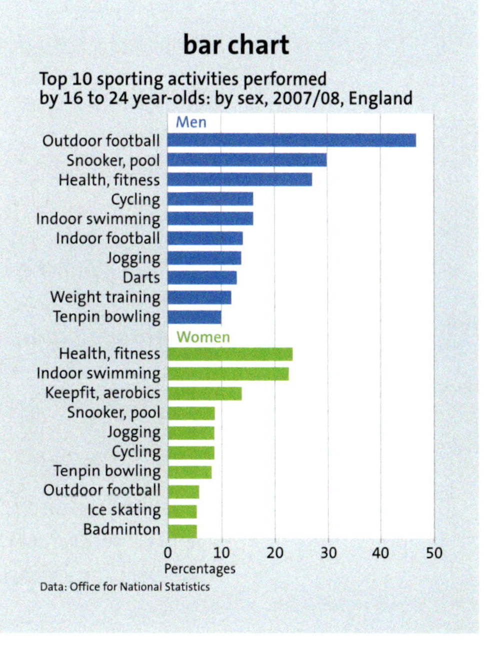

pie chart

Children's expenditure on selected items, 2006/07, United Kingdom

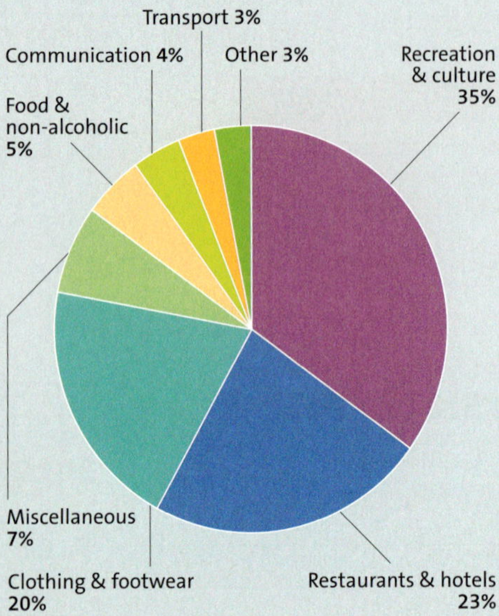

Data: Office for National Statistics

table

Table 1 Percentage of students at each proficiency level on the science scale

	Proficiency levels in science						
	Below Level 1	Level 1	Level 2	Level 3	Level 4	Level 5	Level 6
Finland	0,5	3,6	13,6	29,1	32,2	17,0	3,9
Estonia	1,0	6,7	21,0	33,7	26,2	10,1	1,4
Hong Kong-China	1,7	7,0	16,9	28,7	29,7	13,9	2,1
Canada	2,2,	7,8	19,1	28,8	27,7	12,0	2,4
Macao-China	1,4	8,9	26,0	35,7	22,8	5,0	0,3
Korea	2,5	8,7	21,2	31,8	25,5	9,2	1,1
Chinese Taipei	1,9	9,7	18,6	27,3	27,9	12,9	1,7
Japan	3,2	8,9	18,5	27,5	27,0	12,4	2,6
Australia	3,0	9,8	20,2	27,7	24,6	11,8	2,8
Liechtenstein	2,6	10,3	21,0	28,7	25,2	10,0	2,2
Netherlands	2,3	10,7	21,1	26,9	25,8	11,5	1,7
New Zealand	4,0	9,7	19,7	25,1	23,9	13,6	4,0
Slovenia	2,8	11,1	23,1	27,6	22,5	10,7	2,2
Hungary	2,7	12,3	26,0	31,1	21,0	6,2	0,6
Germany	4,1	11,3	21,4	27,9	23,6	10,0	1,8
Ireland	3,5	12,0	24,0	29,7	21,4	8,3	1,1
Czech Republic	3,5	12,1	23,4	27,8	21,7	9,8	1,8
Switzerland	4,5	11,6	21,8	28,2	23,5	9,1	1,4
Austria	4,3	12,0	21,8	28,3	23,6	8,8	1,1
Sweden	3,8	12,6	25,2	29,5	21,1	6,8	1,1
United Kingdom	4,8	11,9	21,8	25,9	21,8	10,9	2,9

Data: Office for National Statistics

In der Klausur – oder Abituraufgabe kann ein **Sachtext mit einer Statistik kombiniert** werden, die in der Analyse zueinander in Beziehung gesetzt werden sollen. Bevor dies geschehen kann, erfolgt zunächst die Analyse und Interpretation der visuellen Darstellung.

Folgende Struktur sollte eingehalten werden:

1. Einleitung:
- Quelle/Fundstelle
- Publikationsjahr
- Art der Darstellung (pie/bar chart; table; line graph)
- Thema
- behandelter Zeitraum

2. Beschreibung/Analyse/Interpretation:
- formale Komponenten (z. B. *horizontal and vertical axis; percentages; absolute numbers*)
- Inhalte (z. B. Entwicklungen; Höhepunkte; Beziehungen zwischen Daten)

3. Schlussfolgerung/Bewertung:
- **zusammenfassende Schlussfolgerung** aus dem Datenmaterial (evtl. unter Einbeziehung von Hintergrundwissen)
- **Bewertung der Quelle** (Verlässlichkeit?; Gefahr der Manipulation?; Einseitigkeit?; Aktualität?)

Improve your text – Useful phrases

1. Introduction
   The **source** of the given pie chart is …
   The above table **was published by** … in the year …
   The **topic/subject/theme** of the line graph is the number of children aged 0–15 who were seriously injured or killed in road accidents in the UK between 1994 and 2007.
   The graph **shows/presents/provides information about** … **over a period of** 13 years.

2. Description/analysis/interpretation:
   On the **horizontal axis** the years are generally shown in **steps/periods of** one year but the data from the year 1994–1998 are subsumed. The **vertical axis** shows the number of severe injuries.
   The numbers **increase/rise/go up by** 5 %/ **to** 7000.
   There is **an increase/a rise/growth of** 5 %/ **to** 7000.
   The number **decrease/fall/drop by** 5 %/ **to** 1000.
   There is **a decrease/fall/drop of** 5 %/ **to** 1000.
   The graph shows **a steady growth/decrease in** … **/a sudden drop in** …
   It **reached a peak** in the year …
   Since then the numbers **have remained constant**.
   There has been a **steady/gradual/continual decline/growth of** …
   For pedestrians the likelihood of being killed or severely injured **increases with** age.
   The pie is **subdivided into** five segments which **represent** the various items children spend their pocket money on.
   The pie chart **reveals/shows** that nearly **three out of five** (59 per cent) young people **reported** took part in sport or exercise as a free time activity in 2007/08.
   Nearly **a third/quarter of** young men …
   With nearly 50 %/20 %, outdoor football is the **most/least** common sporting activity chosen by men.
   Restaurants and clothing were the **second and third largest** categories.
   The **smallest/largest segments/sections stand for** …
   The amount of pocket money spent on transport **amounts to/is** 3 %.
   The **majority/minority of** …

3. Conclusion/evaluation
   Taking into account that/Considering …
   Against the background of … these results are/are not very surprising/revealing/shocking …
   The chart obviously tries to **manipulate** the reader by not mentioning/by subsuming … under/neglecting the fact that/ignoring that …
   The table is extremely **biased/one-sided/far from objective** because …

1.8 Wie man bildliche Darstellungen analysiert und interpretiert

74 f. 88 11

- Analyse how the poster illustrates the message conveyed in the editorial.
- Examine whether the cartoon can be regarded as a critical comment on the editorial.

Neben der Kombination eines Sachtextes mit einer Statistik ist im Abitur und in Oberstufenklausuren auch die **Kombination mit einer bildlichen Darstellung** möglich.

Eine Karikatur bezieht zum Beispiel auf eine **pointierte** Art und mit primär **visuellen** Mitteln Stellung zu einem **aktuellen Sachverhalt**. Häufig ist die **Bildunterschrift** (*caption*) wesentlicher Bestandteil der Karikatur. Die in der Karikatur dargestellten Personen des öffentlichen

Lebens sind meist durch eine **übertriebene Darstellung bestimmter körperlicher Besonderheiten** erkennbar.

Die Analyse/Interpretation erfolgt in folgenden Schritten:

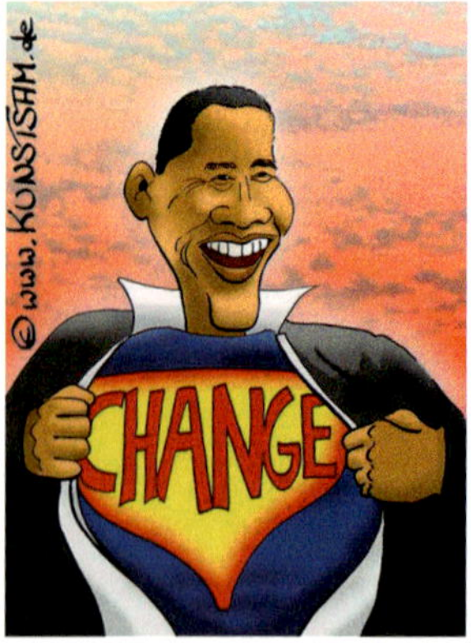

1. Einleitung:
- Thema
- (Karikaturist)
- Publiaktionsort/-datum

2. Detaillierte Beschreibung von Bild und Text

3. Analyse/Interpretation
- Bezug zu (aktuellen) politischen/geschichtlichen Ereignissen/Persönlichkeiten
- Interpretation von Symbolen/Anspielungen
- Analyse der Darstellung der Personen und deren Beziehungen

4. Schlussfolgerung:
- Wirkung der bildlichen Darstellung
- Intention der Darstellung

Improve your text – Useful phrases

1. **Introduction**
   The above cartoon was published in … on …
   It deals with/is about/refers to/depicts/shows/criticises/illustrates/focuses on/makes fun of …

2. **Detailed description:**
   The pictorial elements of the cartoon can easily be distinguished.
   In the foreground/centre/background … is shown/depicted/can be seen.
   In the top left-hand corner/bottom right-hand corner …
   The caption states/plainly shows that …

3. **Analysis/interpretation:**
   The … refers to/stands for/symbolises/hints at …
   … is meant to criticise …
   It becomes quite clear/obvious that …
   … is depicted as a powerful/egoistical/brutal … man/woman who …
   The relationship between … and … is characterised by hate/understanding/ignorance …
   The caption is unexpected/forms a contrast to the picture.

4. **Conclusion:**
   The cartoon clearly shows that …
   It is plain/obvious that …
   The message of the cartoon is that …
   The cartoonist wants to criticise/make people aware of the fact that/raise awareness of …
   The cartoon makes one think about …/raises the question of whether …

2. Fertigkeiten zur Analyse und Produktion argumentativer Texte

2.1 Wie man die Argumentationsstruktur (*composition*) analysiert

44 f. 89 1

- Analyse how the author conveys her idea of the American Dream. Consider **composition** and language.

Eine klare Argumentationsstruktur erleichtert zum einen das Nachvollziehen der im Text oder in der Rede geäußerten Gedanken. Zum anderen dient sie aber durchaus auch der Manipulation: Wenn etwas logisch und durchdacht klingt, sind wir in der Regel geneigt, es zu glauben. Die Analyse des Textaufbaus ist somit unter anderem ein Instrumentarium, das es uns erlaubt, Manipulationsversuche seitens des Redners oder des Autors aufzudecken.

Wie ist der Text strukturiert?

- Wie ist die **Einleitung** gestaltet? Wird schon hier eine **klare Position** bezogen/**These** formuliert, die dann **begründet/untermauert** wird?
- Enthält der Text mehrere **Thesen** oder nur eine?
- Welche ***connectives*** geben Aufschluss über die Struktur des Textes (Gegensätze, Vergleiche, Fakten vs. persönliche Meinung etc.)?
- Werden gegensätzliche Phänomene/Positionen/Zeitpunkte/Schlussfolgerungen einander **gegenübergestellt** bzw. direkt oder indirekt **verglichen**?
- Was fällt bei der **Anordnung der Argumente** auf? Nennt der Autor/Redner **viele** Argumente, um seine Meinung zu untermauern oder baut er auf **wenige**, aber dafür **sehr überzeugende**?
- Sind die Argumente mit **Beispielen** illustriert?
- Werden erst **Gegenargumente** genannt, die dann widerlegt werden?
- Ist eine **Veränderung im Grad der Distanziertheit** zu bemerken (z. B. von sachlich distanziert zu polemisch involviert)?
- Gibt es ein **Thema/Motiv**, auf das immer wieder zurückgegriffen wird?
- Worin besteht die **Zusammenfassung/das Fazit** des Textes? Wo liegt der **Schwerpunkt**?

The flag of freedom has been flying low in recent years. Our traditional institutions and liberties have been traduced by a Government which despises our past. Our democracy has been grievously weakened by the transfer of sovereignty to an unelected bureaucracy in Brussels. Our individual rights have been undermined by arrogant officials, constantly prying into our lives or grabbing our money.

introduction = thesis: British government ignores valuable historical achievements
1. democracy: → growing influence of EU
2. liberty: → deprivation of individual rights

But at last there is a mood of rebellion in the air against the increasingly authoritarian State machine. In Ireland the public refused to be bullied into supporting the Lisbon Treaty […].
Here in Britain the resignation of Shadow Home Secretary David Davis represents another trumpet blast against the creeping despotism of the State. Davis decided to give up his seat and fight a by-election campaign in defence of our civil liberties after Labour forced through its scheme to extend the legal detention period for terror suspects to 42 days.

reference to concrete events that indirectly support thesis: Other people also feel like the author
1. growing influence of EU: Ireland's refusal to support an EU treaty
2. deprivation of individual rights: protest against a Labour decision concerning detention of terror suspects

[…] In New Labour's brave new world the relationship between the citizen and the State has completely altered. In a true democracy the State should be accountable to the public but today law-abiding people are increasingly being told to account for their actions by a vast army of tax collectors, recycling inspectors, municipal pen pushers, civil servants, traffic attendants, diversity enforcers and police officers.

reinforcement of thesis by focussing on relationship state-citizens: it has been perverted
contrast: true democracy ≠ today's state (again reference to the past): State is supposed to justify its actions, not the citizens

[…] This is an administration that has lost all concept of the real meaning of terms like freedom, democracy or liberty. It blathers about "empowerment" and "Britishness" but it destroys our national identity and freedoms. In place of progress it fosters a climate of fear for its own ends.

Leo McKinstry, Daily Express, June 16, 2008

conclusion: repetition of thesis; criticism of government (promises ≠ actions)
→ negative outlook on future

2.2 Wie man rhetorische Mittel erkennt und ihre Wirkung beschreibt

48 f. 90 3 f.; 11

- Examine how the author tries to convince his readers. Refer to the use of language and the **argumentative techniques/rhetorical devices** he employs.

Noch eindeutiger als die Argumentationsstruktur dient die Verwendung rhetorischer Mittel der Manipulation des Lesers oder Zuhörers. Die Analyse hilft, sich von der Position des Autors oder Redners zu distanzieren und zu einer eigenen Meinung zu finden.

Folgende rhetorische Mittel können in einem Sachtext vorkommen:

rhetorische Mittel	mögliche Funktionen/Wirkungen	
repetition (to repeat) – **anaphora** ("When we … when we … when we …") – **alliteration** ("So soft, so sweet …") – **parallelism/gradation** ("I like chocolate, I love chocolate, I crave chocolate.")	– to stress/to put emphasis on/to emphasise/to draw attention to … key words/major arguments/important aspects – increase in intensity	Hervorheben
use of first person plural pronoun ("We all agree …")	– to involve the listeners/readers – speaker presumes/presupposes that listeners/readers support his/her point of view/agree with him/her (It seems unreasonable not to agree with the speaker.) – speaker wants to impose his/her opinion on the reader – to create the illusion of a group identity/mutual understanding (against "them")	Einbeziehen
directly addressing the listeners/readers ("Would you want to…")	– to make them feel involved – to appeal to the listeners'/readers' conscience	
rhetorical question ("Do you really believe that …?")	– to involve listeners/readers – to make them think or question old beliefs – to arouse interest/to attract attention	
drastic/vivid descriptions ("Having seen people jump off the building …")	– to appeal to … – … emotions rather than to reason – … the listeners'/readers' conscience	Illustrieren/Emotionen wecken
enumeration (to enumerate) ("The problems are caused by our cars, our electronic devices and our factories.")	– to emphasise/to stress sth. – to make listeners/readers aware of the extent of the problem – to convey an increase in intensity	
comparison/simile (to compare sth. to/with sth.) ("You are blind as a bat.")	– to arouse interest – to simplify complicated matters by referring to everyday/known experiences/phenomena	
personification (to personify) ("The USA bears responsibility …")	– to simplify matters by reducing complexity – to imply that the abstract unit/phenomenon can (re)act as a unit	
metaphor (for)/**image/symbol** (of)	– to arouse interest – to simplify – to illustrate	
irony/sarcasm	– indirect criticism	
hyperbole/exaggeration ("Nobody who is right in their head would dare to suggest …")	– to launch into a polemic – to stress/to highlight a fact	
claims (instead of well-balanced arguments) ("No one can seriously deny that global warming is caused by humans.")	– no room left for doubts/questions – speaker presumes that listeners/readers agree with him/her (appeal to general knowledge/common sense)	Absichern
to quote experts/authorities; to refer to statistics/polls/research	– to back up/support one's own arguments – to eliminate doubt	

Improve your text – Useful phrases

- In order to convince the readers/the audience of his opinion, the author/speaker makes use of several rhetorical devices.
- By employing/using an anaphora, the author underlines/stresses/emphasises …
- The metaphor in line … suggests that/illustrates that/expresses that …
- In the … line the author makes fun of/refers to/describes/quotes …
- The personification of … suggests that/makes it clear that/shows that …

The flag of freedom has been flying low in recent years.

metaphor: vivid illustration of author's perception; attracts attention and evokes patriotic feelings

Our traditional institutions and liberties have been traduced by a Government which despises our past.

parallel structure: emphasis (severe changes in Britain both for democracy and the individual)

Our democracy has been grievously weakened by the transfer of sovereignty to an unelected bureaucracy in Brussels.

Our individual rights have been undermined by arrogant officials, constantly prying into our lives or grabbing our money.

But at last there is a mood of rebellion in the air against the increasingly authoritarian State machine.

metaphor: mood of rebellion can be noticed everywhere;
metaphor: comparison with machine; association: emotionless; merciless; inhumane

[…] In New Labour's brave new world the relationship between the citizen and the State has completely altered. In a true democracy the State should be accountable to the public but today law-abiding people are increasingly being told to account for their actions by a vast army of tax collectors […]

repetition of "account": contrast and perversion is stressed
allusion to Huxley's dystopian novel

Leo McKinstry, Daily Express, June 16, 2008

Nachdem man den Text auf die rhetorischen Mittel hin untersucht hat, kommt es darauf an, sie **gemäß ihrem Effekt zu** kategorisieren (→ S. 12) und eine in sich schlüssige und logisch strukturierte Analyse zu schreiben.

The author tries to involve the readers. For example he asks rhetorical questions (cf. l. 3; l. 4) to make them think about the issue of racism and to make them aware of the fact that he or she might be racist themselves. Moreover, he uses the first person plural pronoun (cf. l. 6; l. 7) presupposing a mutual understanding and thereby alienating everybody who is of a different opinion.
Appealing to his readers' emotions is another effective way of convincing them. In line 6 for example, he describes concrete consequences of racism very vividly …

2.3 Wie man argumentative Texte schreibt

91

- Write a short **speech** to be held in class in which you refer to the above article and argue from the perspective of a German immigrant.
- **Discuss** the author's thesis that genetic engineering offers "great opportunities for the creation of a happy future for everybody" (l. 7).

In einem argumentativen Text (Rede, Kommentar) nimmt man **Stellung zu einer bestimmten Frage oder Problematik** und möchte andere durch **nachvollziehbare Argumente und konkrete Beispiele** von der eigenen Haltung **überzeugen**.

Da es beim Verfassen eines argumentativen Textes auf eine möglichst gelungene **Verknüpfung von Sprache, Inhalt und Form** ankommt, bedarf es einer gewissenhaften Vorbereitung.

Folgende Schritte können für die Vorbereitung des Schreibprozesses hilfreich sein:

1. Entscheidung für einen Standpunkt
2. Sammeln von Argumenten, die diesen Standpunkt untermauern
3. Je nach Aufgabenstellung und gewünschter Struktur des argumentativen Textes: Sammeln von Argumenten, die dem eigenen Standpunkt entgegengehalten werden könnten.
4. Festlegung einer günstigen Reihenfolge der Argumente
   - zunächst die Argumente, die die eigene Position widerlegen könnten
   - dann die Argumente, die die eigene Position unterstützen; vom **schwächsten zum stärksten Argument**
5. Suche von Beispielen, mit denen die einzelnen Argumente gewinnbringend illustriert werden können
6. Entscheidung für eine **pointierte Einleitung** des argumentativen Textes: Zitat; rhetorische Frage; Fakten
7. Erstellen einer schriftlichen Gliederung: Achte darauf, dass du pro Argument einen neuen Abschnitt beginnst (→ S. 13)!

1. introduction
2. development
   2.1. my own point of view
   [2.2. arguments for the opposite point of view]
   2.3. arguments for my point of view
      2.3.1. argument no. 1 (weakest argument)
         2.3.1.1. topic sentence
         2.3.1.2. explanation and examples [...]
      2.3.4. argument no. 4 (strongest argument)
         2.3.4.1. topic sentence
         2.3.4.2. explanation and examples
3. conclusion

Während des Schreibprozesses müssen die einzelnen Gedanken und Abschnitte logisch durch ***connectives*** verknüpft werden (→ S. 14). Je nach Arbeitsauftrag können (Leserbrief; Diskussion; Kommentar) oder müssen (Rede) **rhetorische Mittel** (→ S. 23) verwendet werden, um die Überzeugungskraft noch zu steigern. Vor allem muss aber durchgängig gewährleistet sein, dass die Leser und Zuhörer sich angesprochen fühlen und den roten Faden nicht verlieren.

Improve your text – Useful phrases

1. **Introduction:**

It is generally believed that …
Most people think that …
At first glance this statement seems to be true.

2. **Development:**

2.1. your point of view: I am of the opinion that …

2.2. arguments for the opposite point of view
It might be argued that …
One could well say that …
It is generally accepted that …
There is some evidence which suggests that …

2.3. arguments for your own point of view
Nevertheless …
However …
It is only partly true that …
Although …
Every argument has two sides.
Take for example …
You have to consider that …
It is often said … but I think …

Everybody must agree that …
Let us now return to …

This brings me to the next point.
A further point to consider is …
We have to admit that …
It is important to realize that …
In addition to this point I want to stress that …
Moreover …
There can be no doubt that …
Everybody knows that this is the case.

3. **Conclusion:**

In conclusion, ...
All in all, ...
It is for these reasons that I believe that ...
Therefore, all in all, I believe that ...

2.4 Wie man Leserbriefe verfasst

74 f. 92 12

- Write a **letter to the editor** in response to this article commenting on the author's opinion on closing Guantanamo.

In einem Leserbrief äußert man seine **Meinung zu einem Zeitungsartikel**. Es handelt sich um eine Sonderform des **formalen** Briefes und um einen **argumentativen Text** (→ S. 25 f.).

Absender ohne Namen

Empfängeradresse

34 Bloomsbury Square
London W8F3BW

Guardian News and Media Ltd
119 Farringdon Road
London
EC1R 3ER

6 July 2009/6th July 2009

Sir or Madam,

Anrede ohne "Dear"

Zeitungsartikel auf den Bezug genommen wird

I have read your article "Closing Guantanamo makes us all safer" (6 July 2009) and I am really shocked/totally agree.

I completely agree with you …
It is quite beyond doubt that …
There is absolutely no point in …
It is not necessarily true that …
The way I see it …
What we have to keep in mind is …
This will raise the question of/whether …

begründete Darlegung der eigenen Meinung

Therefore, we should be careful not to …
That is why I absolutely support your view of the matter/oppose your point of view.

Mary Ecclesby, London

Briefende: Name, Wohnort (keine Grußformel!)

3. Fertigkeiten zur Analyse und Produktion fiktionaler Texte

3.1 Wie man Gedichte analysiert

80 f. 93 15

- Analyse the speaker's mood and the atmosphere conveyed in the poem.
- Examine the imagery used in the sonnet.

Der **Inhalt und die Intention** eines Gedichts erschließen sich meist nur – oder zumindest besser – wenn man es genauer analysiert hat. **Wie bei keinem anderen Text sind nämlich im Gedicht Inhalt und Form miteinander verwoben.**

- Klassischerweise besteht ein Gedicht aus verschiedenen **Strophen (*stanzas*)**, die sich wiederum aus **Versen (*lines*)** zusammensetzen, die sich **reimen (*to rhyme*)** können. Manchmal gibt es auch einen **Refrain (*chorus*)**. Die **Sonette Shakespeares** weisen eine ganz spezielle Struktur auf (→ S. 77)
- Weiterhin typisch für Gedichte ist die Verwendung von **Bildern und Vergleichen** (***imagery***; vgl. Liste auf der nächsten Seite).
- Auch der **Klang und Rhythmus** eines Gedichts sind eng mit seinem Inhalt verknüpft: Wiederholungen, Alliterationen und Anaphern tragen zur Vermittlung einer bestimmten Stimmung bei (vgl. Liste auf der nächsten Seite).

Folgende Fragen können bei der Gedichtanalyse hilfreich sein:

1. Wie ist das Gedicht strukturiert?

- Aus wie vielen Strophen besteht das Gedicht? Worum geht es in den Strophen? Gibt es einen Refrain oder einen wiederkehrenden Vers, der das Thema angibt?

2. Welche Stimmung wird durch den Klang und den Rhythmus erzeugt?

- Hat das Gedicht einen **gleichmäßigen oder ungleichmäßigen** Rhythmus? Je nachdem wird eine eher heitere/lebendige/chaotische etc. oder eine melancholische/traurige/harmonische etc. Stimmung/Atmosphäre erzeugt.
- Dominieren **dunkle oder helle Vokale**? Werden diese durch Alliterationen oder Reime besonders betont? Auch hierdurch wird entweder eine eher heitere, helle oder bedrohlich dunkle Atmosphäre hervorgerufen.

3. Welche Bilder werden verwendet?

- Aus welchem Bereich stammen die Bilder (z. B. Natur; Alltag; Krieg …)?
- Was bedeuten sie, wenn man sie wörtlich nimmt? Was verbindet man mit ihnen? Was könnten sie – im Gesamtzusammenhang des Gedichts – im übertragenen Sinn bedeuten?

4. Was fällt bei der Wortwahl auf?

- Werden **viele Adjektive** verwendet? Wenn ja, handelt es sich wahrscheinlich um ein beschreibendes Gedicht, das dem Leser etwas vor dem inneren Auge ausmalen will; die Sinne werden angesprochen; es ist ein **Gemälde mit Worten**.
- Werden **viele Verben** verwendet? Wenn ja, kann das Gedicht je nach Verben sehr **lebendig** oder auch **statisch** wirken; vielleicht wird auch ein Kontrast hergestellt zwischen lebendigen und statischen/passiven Aspekten.
- Welche Wörter werden wiederholt (*anaphora*)? Welche Wirkung hat das?

Folgende Stilmittel können in einem Gedicht vorkommen:

Stilmittel	Erklärung	Beispiele aus Gedichten	mögliche Wirkungen/Funktionen
alliteration	**repetition of a consonant** at the beginning of neighbouring words, or of stressed syllables within such words	I caught this morning morning's minion (G. M. Hopkins, *The Windhover*)	– to produce a rhythmic effect – comic effect – onomatopoeia
anaphora	**repetition of the same words** in neighbouring stanzas, lines etc. usually at the beginning.	*And* I saw it was filled with graves, *and* tomb stones where flowers should be: *and* priests in black gowns (W. Blake, *The Garden of Love*)	– to stress a certain aspect – to drum sth. into the listener/ reader – the fact cannot be ignored
enjambment	sentence or a clause in a poem which **runs on from one line to the next** without a pause (also called run-on-line)	And, when there came a pause Of silence such as baffled his best skill (W. Wordsworth, *There was a boy*)	– to enact meaning (cp. example) – creation of suspense, surprise
gradation parallel structure	A number of statements are ordered in a series so that each one rises above the one preceding, leading to a climax. **Repetition and parallel structures** are normally characteristic of gradation.	*We shall learn* all these devices the white man has, *We shall handle* his tools for ourselves. *We shall master* his machinery, his inventions (D. Nez, *New Way, Old Way*)	– emphasis
metaphor, metaphorical	Two seemingly unlike things are linked with one another in the form of an **implicit comparison**.	There's daggers in men's smiles (W. Shakespeare, *Macbeth*, II. iii, 147)	– to convey feelings that cannot be described – reader has to think twice – image can convey many different aspects – to offer new insights into the object of discussion
metre	regular arrangement of strong stresses in a stretch of language; **group of stressed and unstressed syllables forms a metrical unit (foot)** – iamb, iambic _X – trochee, trochaic X_ – dactyl X_ _ – anapaest _ _X	 event, avoid happen, woman happily, elements underneath	– underlines general atmosphere conveyed by the poem: – regular metre: peaceful, calm, controlled, dull, boring … – irregular metre: chaotic, creative, disturbing, hectic …

Stilmittel	Erklärung	Beispiele aus Gedichten	mögliche Wirkungen/Funktionen
onomatopoeia onomatopoeic	use of words which **imitate the sounds** they refer to	buzz, cuckoo, smack	– vivid illustration – appeal to sense of hearing
oxymoron	**combination of two contrary terms**	the <u>*gentle hammer blow*</u> of her kisses (B. Cole, *Reported Missing*)	– emphasis – reader has to think twice – sth. is beyond reasoning and everyday experience
personification to personify	representing animals, plants, objects, abstract ideas **as if they were human beings and possessed human qualities**	See the mountains kiss high Heaven And the waves clasp one another (P. B. Shelley, *Love's Philosophy*)	– to depict nature etc. from a different perspective – to arouse the reader's awareness – to open the reader's eyes to new experiences
repetition	**repeated use** of particular sounds, syllables, words, phrases, sentences	He was <u>*my*</u> North, <u>*my*</u> South, <u>*my*</u> East and West, <u>*My*</u> working week and <u>*my*</u> Sunday rest (W. H. Auden, *Funeral Blues*)	– to structure the poem – to stress keywords – emphasis
rhetorical questions	writer expects the reader to know and be **totally convinced of the appropriate reply to the question**	Have I not passed thee on the wooden bridge, Wrapped in thy cloak and battling with the snow? (M. Arnold, *The Scholar Gipsy*)	– emphasis – to raise tension
rhyme alternate rhyme enclosed rhyme	a b a b a b b a		– to achieve a pleasant sound – to underline the structure of a poem – to link two words together
simile	**explicit comparison** through the words *as* or *like*	Love is <u>*like a flower*</u>, it must flower and fade (D. H. Lawrence, *The Mess of Love*)	– to offer new insights into the object of discussion
symbol, symbolic(al)	The concrete object not only stands for itself but also for some **abstract idea**. Symbols exist by **tradition and convention**.	lion: rose: white: green/spring: black/winter:	– symbol of power – symbol of love – symbol of innocence – symbol of a new beginning – symbol of death

Manchmal ist in der Aufgabenstellung ein **Schwerpunkt der Analyse** (z. B. *imagery* oder *composition*) vorgegeben.
Beim Schreibprozess ist auf eine **nachvollziehbare Struktur** (→ S. 13 f.) und ausreichende **Textbelege** (→ S. 15 f.) zu achten.

Improve your text – Useful phrases

- The poem "…" by xy is about/deals with/intends to make the reader consider …
- It consists of … stanzas with … lines each.
- The poet conveys a sad/uncanny … atmosphere by employing/using a range of stylistic devices.
- By using … the author stresses/underlines/emphasises/puts emphasis on …
- The … suggests/expresses/illustrates/supports/shows/indicates that …

3.2 Wie man das *setting* eines fiktionalen Textes analysiert

58 f. 94 5

- Analyse how the setting described at the beginning contributes to the overall atmosphere conveyed in the story.
- Examine how the setting mirrors the mood of the main character.

Meist zu Beginn jeder Kurzgeschichte, jedes Dramas und jedes Romans wird das sogenannte *setting* beschrieben bzw. vorgestellt.

setting = Ort und Zeit

In der Analyse des *settings* soll deutlich werden, wie die direkte oder indirekte Beschreibung von Ort und Zeit zur Schaffung einer bestimmten **Atmosphäre (*atmosphere*)** beiträgt, die **Stimmungen/Gefühle der literarischen Figuren** widerspiegelt oder kontrastiert und/oder das Thema des Textes einleitet bzw. illustriert.

The Pedestrian
by Ray Bradbury

To enter out into that silence that was the city at eight o'clock of a misty evening in November, to put your feet upon that buckling concrete walk, to step over grassy seams and make your way, hands in pockets, through the silences, that was what Mr Leonard Mead most dearly loved to do. […] he was alone in this world of 2053 A.D., or as good as alone, and with a final decision made, a path selected, he would stride off, sending patterns of frosty air before him like the smoke of a cigar. Sometimes he would walk for hours and miles and return only at midnight to his house. And on his way he would see the cottages and homes with their dark windows, and it was not unequal to walking through a graveyard where only the faintest glimmers of firefly light appeared in flickers behind the windows. Sudden gray phantoms seemed to manifest upon inner room walls where a curtain was still undrawn against the night, or there were whisperings and murmurs where a window in a tomb-like building was still open. […]

Ray Bradbury, *The Pedestrian*, in: The Reporter (7. August 1951), p. 55

Setting

basic information: a city in the future (2053) on a November evening

atmosphere

in general: cold, quiet, dark

- no people on the streets; they are sitting at home → deserted place
- protagonist is an exception ("alone", l. 7)

graveyard imagery: walking down the road is like walking in a dark cemetery only faintly illuminated ("faintest glimmers of firefly light", l. 15 f.); houses like tombs; people are "gray phantoms", l. 17, they whisper and murmur

description of pavement: not well cared for ("buckling", l. 3, "grassy seams", l. 4) → not used very often

What does the description of the setting tell us about the society the protagonist lives in?

emotionally cold world; gloomy atmosphere; people are like the living dead (no joy in life); trapped in their houses; being outside is not an option for whatever reason (only for some loners such as the protagonist); protagonist is exceptional (hero in a dystopian world?)

Improve your text – Useful phrases

- The story is set in …
- There are various hints which suggest that …
- That narrator gives a rough/detailed/vivid impression of the room/the town/the street …
- The atmosphere conveyed underlines/mirrors/forms an effective contrast to the protagonist's situation/feelings …
- The word(s) … in l. … suggest that/imply/convey an … atmosphere/conjure up the impression of …
- What is striking here is …/This makes the reader think of …
- All things considered, there is evidence enough to say that …
- All in all, we can conclude that the narrator wants to convey that …

Manchmal ist ein **Schwerpunkt der Analyse** (z. B. *effect of sounds* oder *contrast of light and darkness*) vorgegeben. Beim Schreibprozess ist auf eine **nachvollziehbare Struktur** (→ S. 13 f.) und ausreichende **Textbelege** (→ S. 15 f.) zu achten.

3.3 Wie man Erzählperspektiven erkennt und ihre Wirkung beschreibt

70 f. 95 9

- Analyse how the atmosphere is conveyed. Focus on the narrative perspective.
- Analyse how the narrative perspective contributes to the overall effect of this excerpt.

Ein narrativer Text lebt von seiner **Erzählperspektive**. Dementsprechend ist die Analyse dieser Perspektive wichtig um die **Wirkung** zu verstehen, die der Text auf uns als Leserinnen und Leser ausübt. Durch die Erzählperspektive werden wir entweder **in die erzählte Welt der Geschichte hineingezogen** und zur **Identifikation** mit einer der literarischen Figuren angeregt oder aber wir werden **auf Distanz gehalten** und damit indirekt zu einer kritischen Beurteilung der dargestellten Situation aufgefordert.

Folgende Erzählperspektiven werden unterschieden:

	Erzählperspektive	Beispiel	mögliche Wirkungen/Funktionsweisen
First person point of view	**first-person narrator** **use of first-person pronoun** Der **Erzähler ist Teil der Geschichte** (*protagonist; minor character*) und erzählt alle Geschehnisse aus seiner Perspektive. Je nach Gemütszustand und Charaktereigenschaften kann er ***reliable*** oder ***unreliable*** sein.	During the whole of a dull, dark, and soundless day in the autumn of the year, when the clouds hung oppressively low in the heavens, I had been passing alone, on horseback, through a singularly dreary tract of country; and at length found myself, as the shades of evening drew on, within view of the melancholy House of Usher. I know not how it was—but, with the first glimpse of the building, a sense of insufferable gloom pervaded my spirit. […] E. A. Poe, *The Fall of the House of Usher*	From the beginning the reader gets all impressions and information filtered through the protagonist's mind. Tension is created because everything is witnessed by the reader from within the protagonist's mind. We do not know more than this character (e. g. characteristics of the setting are only gradually revealed; it's like solving a riddle/doing a jigsaw puzzle). The reader is made curious; s/he would like to know more than the protagonist.

	Erzählperspektive	Beispiel	mögliche Wirkungen/Funktionsweisen
First person point of view	**stream of consciousness** Wir als Leser und Leserinnen tauchen gleichsam in den **Gedankenstrom einer der literarischen Figuren** ein und erleben alles durch diese Figur.	[…] AT LEAST THAT IF NO MORE, thought through my eyes. Signatures of all things I am here to read, seaspawn and seawrack, the nearing tide, that rusty boot. Snotgreen, bluesilver, rust: coloured signs. Limits of the diaphane. But he adds: in bodies. Then he was aware of them bodies before of them coloured. How? By knocking his sconce against them, sure. […] J. Joyce, *Ulysses*	The reader is drawn into the atmosphere of the setting/invited to feel and see what the protagonist sees and feels; thus a closeness between reader and protagonist is established; the reader witnesses everything with a great deal of immediacy. The other characters are described from one character's perspective (subjective!), so it becomes clear that s/he likes/hates/ suspects …
Third person point of view	**third-person limited narrator** **third-person limited point of view** Die Handlung wird **aus der Perspektive einer der literarischen Figuren** erzählt, obwohl auf sie mit den **Pronomen *he/she*** rekurriert wird. So lernen wir als Leser und Leserinnen eine bestimmte subjektive Sicht kennen ohne uns aber vollkommen mit ihr zu identifizieren, da durch das Pronomen eine Distanz erhalten bleibt.	Parker's wife was sitting on the front porch floor, snapping beans. Parker was sitting on the steep, some distance away, watching her sullenly. She was plain, plain. The skin on her face was thin and drawn as tight as the skin on an onion and her eyes were gray and sharp like the points of two icepicks. Parker understood why he had married her – he couldn't have got her any other way – but he couldn't understand why he stayed with her now. She was pregnant and pregnant women were not his favorite kind. […] Sometimes he supposed that she had married him because she meant to save him […] F. O'Connor, *Parker's Back*	(Viele Wirkungen/Funktionsweisen des *first-person point of view* treffen hier auch zu.) A closeness between the reader and the character is established, but as the third person pronoun is used a certain distance remains. The descriptions are restricted/limited to one character's perspective. The events are viewed from a subjective angle. Because of the perspective taken the reader gets insights into the character's motivation and attitudes.
	omniscient narrator **omniscient point of view** Der Erzähler bewegt sich **frei in Raum und Zeit** und kennt die Gedanken, Motive und Charaktereigenschaften **aller literarischer Figuren**. Manchmal **wertet und kommentiert** er Personen und Handlungen.	There was a woman who was beautiful, who started with all the advantages, yet she had no luck. She married for love, and the love turned to dust. She had bonny children, yet she felt they had been thrust upon her, and she could not love them. They looked at her coldly, as if they were finding fault with her. And hurriedly she felt she must cover up some fault in herself. Yet what it was that she must cover up she never knew. Nevertheless, when her children were present, she always felt the centre of her heart go hard. […] Everybody else said of her: "She is such a good mother. She adores her children." Only she herself, and her children themselves, knew it was not so. They read it in each other's eyes. […] D. H. Lawrence, *The Rocking-Horse Winner*	The narrator himself does not participate in the action but describes the actions of all characters without focusing on one point of view. The fact that he knows details about … also shows that he is omniscient. He has complete insight into the characters' thoughts, motivations and emotions and therefore offers direct characterisation. He provides the readers with his comments and evaluations. Every single piece of information given to the reader is already interpreted by the omniscient narrator. He describes what the various characters are doing simultaneously and thereby gives the reader the opportunity to compare their behaviour.

3.4 Wie man literarische Figuren charakterisiert

62 f. 96 7

- Characterise the protagonist, focusing on his behaviour towards his wife and his daughter.

Um eine literarische Figur zu charakterisieren, muss man zunächst möglichst viele Informationen zu folgenden Aspekte sammeln.

- **Eckdaten** (Alter, Beruf, Familie …)

- **äußeres Erscheinungsbild** (*outward appearance*)

- **Haltungen/Wünsche/allgemeine Eigenschaften**

- **Verhalten in bestimmten Situationen**

- **Verhalten/Gefühle gegenüber anderen**

- **persönliche Entwicklung (Krisen; Wendepunkte)**

Diese Aspekte werden zuweilen **direkt** vom Erzähler genannt (***direct characterisation, telling***).

> With despair – cold, sharp despair – buried deep in her heart like a wicked knife, Miss Meadows, in cap and gown and carrying a little baton, trod the cold corridors that led to the music hall. […]
>
> K. Mansfield, *The Singing Lesson*

> "Have you really never been to a ball before, Leila? But my child, how too weird –" cried the Sheridan girls. "Our nearest neighbour was fifteen miles," said Leila softly, gently opening and shutting her fan. Oh dear, how hard it was to be indifferent like the others! She tried to smile not too much; she tried not to care. […]
>
> K. Mansfield, *Her First Ball*

In den meisten Fällen müssen sie jedoch **erschlossen** werden, indem man z. B. das Verhalten oder die Gedanken der zu charakterisierenden Figur analysiert und deutet. (***indirect characterisation; showing***)

Folgende Schritte können beim Anfertigen einer Charakterisierung hilfreich sein:

- Der Text(auszug) wird aufmerksam durchgelesen und es werden die Stellen **unterstrichen**, die direkt oder indirekt über die literarische Figur Aufschluss geben.
- Am **Rand** können auffällige Charakterzüge bereits **stichpunktartig** notiert werden.
- Zur **Vorstrukturierung** der Charakterisierung und um sicherzustellen, keine wesentlichen Aspekte vergessen zu haben, ist eine Kategorisierung der gesammelten Erkenntnisse in Form einer **Mindmap** (→ S. 12) zu empfehlen (einschließlich wichtiger Textverweise).

- Beim Schreibprozess ist auf eine **nachvollziehbare Struktur** (→ S. 13 f.) und ausreichende **Textbelege** (→ S. 15 f.) zu achten. Es ist sinnvoll vom äußeren Erscheinungsbild auszugehen, um dann (je nach Schwerpunkt der Aufgabenstellung) auf andere wesentliche Eigenschaften einzugehen.

Improve your text – Useful phrases

- The main character/protagonist in the story is …
- The narrator describes/characterises him/her as …
- … is mainly characterised by his selfishness/arrogance/insecurity …
- His/her behaviour is marked by arrogance/insecurity/self-confidence.
- She/he behaves in a … way. This becomes obvious in l. … when she/he says that …
- His/her indifference/love/hate … becomes apparent when he …
- This behaviour shows that she/he is …/Here it becomes obvious/clear that she/he is …
- When saying that … she/he reveals that she/he is/feels …
- She/he always (re)acts spontaneously/cleverly/quickly …
- She/he seems to be someone who …
- In lines … it becomes obvious that she/he likes/dislikes/hates/enjoys …
- She/he gradually develops into a mature/caring/frustrated/resigned … person.
- In contrast to … she/he feels insecure/satisfied/enthusiastic about/scared …

3.5 Wie man kreative Schreibaufträge bearbeitet

67 f.; 70 f. 97 8; 9

- Write the letter referred to in line 4 of this extract.
- Imagine what is going on in the protagonist's mind when she leaves. Write down her thoughts using the first-person point of view.

Bei der dritten Aufgabe in Oberstufen- und Abiturklausuren kann es sich um eine so genannte **produktionsorientierte** Aufgabenstellung handeln. Dies bedeutet, dass hier eine kreative Weiterführung des Textes verlangt wird – in Form eines Tagebucheintrages, eines Briefs, einer Fortführung des Textauszugs, eines Dialogs oder ähnlichem.

Folgende Aspekte sollten beim Bearbeiten einer kreativen Schreibaufgabe beachtet werden:

- Der selbstverfasste Text darf dem Ausgangstext **nicht widersprechen**.
- Er muss alle dem Ausgangstext zu entnehmenden **wesentlichen Details** enthalten.
- Je nach Schreibauftrag muss darauf geachtet werden, dass die **Perspektive** gewahrt bzw. die geforderte Perspektive eingenommen wird. Je nach Perspektive ändert sich die Wahrnehmung der Situation und der literarischen Figuren. Die eingenommene Perspektive wird sich gegebenenfalls auch in Sprachstil und Wortwahl widerspiegeln.
- Der in der Aufgabenstellung genannte **inhaltliche Schwerpunkt** muss beachtet werden.
- Es muss eine der **Textsorte angemessene Sprache** gewählt werden. Ein Tagebucheintrag klingt zum Beispiel anders als ein formaler Brief!
- Die **formalen Kennzeichen der geforderten Textsorte** (Tagebucheintrag, informeller Brief, formaler Brief etc.) müssen beachtet werden.

- Es muss eine der **Situation und dem/den Adressaten angemessene Sprache** gewählt werden. Dem Verfassen eines Dialogs zwischen dem Protagonisten und einer anderen literarischen Figur muss demnach zum Beispiel eine korrekte Einschätzung der entsprechenden Beziehung vorausgegangen sein.

3.6 Wie man Regieanweisungen deutet

☑ 98

- Explain how the scriptwriter uses stage directions to paint a portrait of the protagonist.
- Analyse how the playwright characterises the couple by his stage directions.

Regieanweisungen zeigen den Schauspielern und Schauspielerinnen wie der Autor des Dramas bzw. des Drehbuchs eine bestimmte Rolle angelegt hat. Es werden in der Regel Informationen und Anweisungen zu folgenden Bereichen gegeben:

- Aussehen
- Mimik und Gestik
- Bewegungsabläufen und Handlungen
- Nähe/Distanz zu anderen Figuren
- Tempo
- Gefühlen

Improve your text – Useful phrases

- This might insinuate/indicate/hint at/imply that …
- Here it becomes obvious that …
- This clearly shows that …
- By describing the … the playwright/scriptwriter wants to draw attention to/stress/underline …

Immer wenn wir ein Drama oder ein Drehbuch lesen anstatt uns eine Aufführung bzw. den Film anzusehen, müssen wir die Regieanweisungen zur Deutung der Handlung und der Motivationen und Gefühle der literarischen Figuren heranziehen.

A. Miller, DEATH OF A SALESMAN ACT ONE

From the right, WILLY LOMAN, the Salesman, enters, carrying two large sample cases. The flute plays on. He hears but is not aware of it. He is past sixty years of age […] Even as he crosses the stage to the doorway of the house, his exhaustion is apparent. He unlocks the door, comes into the kitchen, and thankfully lets his burden, down, feeling the soreness of his palms. A word-sigh escapes his lips – it might be "oh, boy, oh, boy." He closes the door, then carries his cases into the living-room, through the draped kitchen doorway.

LINDA, his wife, has stirred in her bed at the right. She gets out and puts on a robe, listening. […]

basic information:
Willy Loman, salesman; about 60
Linda: his wife
late at night or early in the morning

additional information:
Willy moves slowly (exhausted); seems to be overstretched by his job (sample cases described as "burden"; he sighs.)

"escapes his lips" might indicate that he does not want anyone to know how tired he is

close relationship between Willy and his wife: She gets up as soon as she hears him coming; "listening" might imply that she has been worrying about him.

4. Fertigkeiten zur Analyse auditiver und audiovisueller Texte

4.1 Wie man Hörverstehensaufgaben bearbeitet

Je nach Funktion und Absicht des Zuhörens wird man sich auf unterschiedliche Weise mit dem Gehörten auseinandersetzen müssen. Grundsätzlich lassen sich **drei Phasen des Zuhörens** unterscheiden, die je nach Situation und Absicht natürlich eine unterschiedliche Gewichtung haben.

Pre-listening: Eine Erwartungshaltung aufbauen

Normalerweise ergeben sich die Erwartungen an eine Hörsituation ganz automatisch: Man weiß, wie eine Stadtführung aufgebaut ist und worauf man während des Zuhörens besonders achten möchte; man hört sich einen gezielt ausgewählten Podcast an, weil man sich z. B. bestimmte Informationen erhofft; man erwartet, dass in Diskussionen verschiedene Standpunkte eingenommen und verteidigt werden usw. All diese Vorinformationen erleichtern das Verstehen.

- In Prüfungssituationen müssen diese Vorinformationen meist gezielt gegeben werde, z. B. indem man Hörbeispiele durch Texte einleitet. Ein **genaues Lesen solcher Einleitungstexte** ist daher sehr hilfreich für das Verständnis des darauf folgenden Hörtextes. Folgende Fragen können hilfreich sein:
  - **Wer** spricht mit **wem**? (Alter, Geschlecht, Beruf, Beziehung, Nationalität, Anzahl der Sprecher/innen)
  - Was ist das **Thema**? (Vielleicht kannst du Vorwissen aktivieren.)
  - Was erfährt man über die **Situation**? (**formell** – Schule, Radiosendung etc. oder **informell** – Kneipe, Kantine, Bushaltestelle, etc.)
  - Um welche **Art** von Hörtext handelt es sich? (Vortrag, Stadtführung, Durchsage, Diskussion, Alltagsgespräch etc.)
- Man sollte sich vor dem Hören darüber im Klaren sein, welche **Absicht** man mit dem Zuhören verfolgt bzw. was während oder nach dem Hören des Textes erwartet wird. Ein genaues Durchlesen der **Aufgaben vor dem Hören des Textes** ermöglicht es, **gezielt** auf bestimmte Details zu achten.

Die Aufgaben zum Hörtext können folgendermaßen aussehen:

Multiple choice; Kurzfragen zum Text; *true/false/not in the text*, Lückentexe; *matching*; Satzergänzungen

Folgendes ist zu beachten:

Multiple choice: Wenn nicht anders vorgegeben, darf **nur eine Antwort** angekreuzt werden. (Wenn du mehrere ankreuzt, wird die Aufgabe nicht gewertet.) Wenn man sich nicht sicher ist, sollte man auf jeden Fall **lieber irgendeine Antwort als keine Antwort** ankreuzen.

true/false/not in the text: Achte darauf, **ob** die falschen Sätze berichtigt werden sollen. *Not in the text* sollte man nur dann ankreuzen, wenn das angesprochene Thema **überhaupt nicht** im Hörtext erwähnt wird.

matching: Bei diesem Aufgabenformat wird erwartet, dass **man bestimmte im Hörtext enthaltene Informationen einander zuordnet**, z. B. Öffnungszeiten den entsprechenden Institutionen; Lebensläufe den genannten Personen und ähnliches.

Listening: Verstehen, was gemeint ist

Im Kontakt mit Muttersprachlern und/oder im englischsprachigen Ausland wird nur indirekt überprüft, ob wir das Gehörte verstanden haben, z. B. indem wir auf das Gesagte so reagieren, wie wir es für angemessen halten und dafür häufig ein entsprechendes Feedback bekommen.

In einer Prüfungssituation wird das Verständnis jedoch direkt geprüft, indem **während des Hörens** bestimmte **Aufgaben** zu bearbeiten sind, in denen das **Grob – und/oder Detailverständnis** überprüft wird.

- Da man diese Aufgaben ja bereits vor dem Hören durchgelesen hat, weiß man worauf besonders zu achten ist. Die Aufgaben sind in der Regel **chronologisch** geordnet, so dass die benötigten Informationen nacheinander genannt werden. Immer wenn man eine relevante Information hört, sollte man die entsprechende Aufgabe **sofort lösen** (z. B. *true* oder *false* ankreuzen). Im Falle von Unsicherheit kann man sich ein **Fragezeichen notieren**, so dass man beim nochmaligen Hören des Textes weiß, auf welche Informationen man gezielt achten muss.
- Auch wenn man nicht alles auf Anhieb versteht, sollte man **einen kühlen Kopf bewahren und weiter konzentriert zuhören**. Dies ist ganz wichtig, um nicht den roten Faden zu verlieren. In der Regel wird man den **gesamten Text am Ende noch einmal hören**.

Post-listening: Das Gehörte verarbeiten

In einer Hörverstehensüberprüfung werden manchmal **Aufgaben** gestellt, die erst **nach dem vollständigen Hören des Textes** bearbeitet werden können, da sie recht komplex sind und/oder ein Nachdenken über das Gehörte voraussetzen.

4.2 Wie man *stills* analysiert – *camera position, range* und *angle*

70 f. | 99 | 9

- Explain which cinematic devices underline the atmosphere described in the excerpt from the novel.
- Compare how the relationship between the protagonist and his wife is described by narrative and cinematic devices.

Bei der Produktion von Spielfilmen ersetzt die Kamera gleichsam den Erzähler: Die Kameraführung bestimmt die Erzählperspektive. Schon bei der Analyse von Standbildern (*stills*) wird dies deutlich.

Camera position

Beispiel aus *American Beauty*	Bezeichnung	mögliche Wirkungen/Funktionen
	establishing shot	– usually at the beginning of a new scene – comparable to an exposition – introduces the setting
	over-the-shoulder shot	– scene is filmed from behind a character's shoulder – often used to film dialogues – Both characters can be seen but the focus is on the character who we see completely.
	point-of-view shot	– scene is taken from a character's point of view (cf. third-person limited narrator) – tension is created – viewer sees the situation through the eyes of one of the characters and thus tends to identify with him and his view (cf. example: viewer sees father and daughter from somebody else's perspective)
	reverse-angle shot/ reaction shot	– camera shows the opposite view of what the viewer has just seen – might be surprising – the tension that has been created by the point-of-view shot is now resolved (cp. example: viewers see who is actually watching the father and his daughter)

camera range

Beispiel aus *Bowling for Columbine*	Bezeichnung	mögliche Wirkungen/Funktionen
	extreme long shot	– no individuals can be identified – general atmosphere is conveyed – setting is introduced
	long shot	– shows some details (e.g. the faces in the crowd; the banners) – people are not emphasized as individuals – everything is still shown from a distance
	medium long shot/full shot	– is effective in showing the interaction between characters – shot of the whole body/object – distance between characters becomes obvious (insinuates their relationship)
	medium shot	– upper body is shown – character's activity is visible
	close-up	– character's head fills the entire scene – camera range captures the viewers' attention – forces the viewer to concentrate on the individual – focuses on facial expressions – tension is raised/created
	extreme close-up	– shows typical/essential detail – tension is raised/created

Camera angle

Beispiel aus *American Beauty*	Bezeichnung	mögliche Wirkungen/Funktionen
	**straight-on angle**	– no hierarchy is implied – neutral/objective angle
	**high-angle shot**	– shot is taken from a high angle – character seems to be reduced in height and appearance – fear/vulnerability/inferiority/helplessness is underlined – hierarchy is implied – might mirror another character's estimation of this character
	**low-angle shot**	– shot is taken from below eye-level – makes the character appear dominant/threatening/superior/powerful – hierarchy is implied – might mirror another character's estimation of this character

Die Darbietung eines *stills* wird immer in einen Textkontext eingebettet sein – sei es ein Auszug aus einem Drehbuch, einem Roman oder einer Filmkritik. Dementsprechend wird die Analyseaufgabe in der Regel darauf hinauslaufen, beides miteinander in Beziehung zu setzen. Bei der Bearbeitung der Aufgabe muss also die in der Aufgabenstellung enthaltene Fokussierung Berücksichtigung finden.

Beim Schreibprozess ist auf eine nachvollziehbare Struktur (→ S. 13 f.) und Rückbezüge zum *still* zu achten.

Improve your text – Useful phrases

- The still conveys a tranquil/threatening/tense/gloomy … atmosphere.
- The overall effect of this still is to draw the viewer into the atmosphere of the film.
- In the foreground/background/centre you can see …
- The picture shows/reveals/conveys/is dominated by …
- To underline/emphasise/stress/support this effect/impression, xy is shown from a high/low angle …
- The viewer is led to believe that/gets the impression that …
- The viewer's attention is drawn to …/is led from x to y/follows the camera.
- As the protagonist is shown in a close-up, the viewer becomes aware of the fact that …
- By using this camera angle the director succeeds in stressing the antagonist's inferiority/superiority/dominance …

Universal Values and Responsibilities in a Globalised World

1. Sich einen Überblick verschaffen

Globalisation is a phenomenon describing the mutual influence **of economies, cultures, governmental systems and political movements around** the world. This is nothing new. Many of the large empires and religions are examples of globalisation throughout history. **Trade** among countries has caused an **increasing interdependence of the world's economies** in the last few centuries. What is nowadays called globalisation represents an enormous acceleration of this process.

As early as 1962, the Canadian visionary Marshall McLuhan wrote that the electronic age was turning all humanity into a "global tribe", and the term *global village* is attributed to him. This term is misleading, though, because it implies that all the different nations and different peoples with their different cultures have merged into one homogeneous people – this, of course, is a misconception. The world is still full of **heterogeneous cultures, values, religions and life styles** which have been at the centre of many **international conflicts. Economic interests**, though, have always played an **important role in international conflicts**.

Trade can only prosper in a **peaceful and trusting environment** and the larger the conflict, meaning the more nations involved, the more devastating its outcome. This awareness led to the establishment of the **League of Nations after WW I**. Unfortunately, this first institution with the purpose of keeping international peace failed and could not prevent the outbreak of another world war with even worse consequences. Thus, it was obvious by the end of WW II that a similar but more powerful institution was necessary in order to prevent wars. As a consequence, on October 24, **1945**, 51 states ratified the United Nations Charter and equipped the **UN** with instruments that its predecessor lacked. It has a **number of ways in which to intervene in conflicts**, military invention always being the last option:

The UN can
- send negotiators or observers to the country.
- impose sanctions.
- send a peacekeeping force (Blue Helmets).
- agree on military intervention.

Undoubtedly, the **UN** has had **great success** since it was established, and **peacekeeping** is by **no means its only purpose or line of work**. As can be seen from the following institutions – UNHCR (United Nations High Commissioner for Refugees), UNICEF (United Nations Children's Fund), UNESCO (United Nations Educational, Scientific and Cultural Organisation), WHO (World Health Organisation) – the UN tries **to improve people's lives** all around the globe. By doing so, it enables different countries to come together to work hand in hand on certain projects. Surely, this in itself is already a **large step towards a more peaceful world**. This can also be said of the General Assembly in which delegates from 192 countries come together to **solve conflicts by talking** instead of resorting to war. Obviously this has **not always** been **successful**, and the **UN** has been paralysed and **helpless in the face of terrorist attacks, wars** and even **genocides** which could not be prevented.

Today, more than 50 years after its founding, the UN is confronted with similar problems like its predecessor; the instruments it has at hand and its **internal structure** (e.g. the Security Council with its veto power and the underrepresentation of take-off and developing nations) are keeping it from working efficiently. The **need for reform** is evident, but the reform process launched by Kofi Anan, predecessor of Secretary-General Ban Ki-moon, has **come to a standstill**. This is especially **distressing** since the process of globalisation has dramatically changed the world, causing upheavals and conflicts all around the globe in which a **stout mediator** is **badly needed**. The potential benefits of globalisation on an economic, social and cultural level are always at risk if peace cannot prevail over war. One must not forget that the **UN in itself is not an independent autonomous unit**. It can only be successful if its members are willing to cooperate. If the UN stays underfunded, its members reluctant to provide well-equipped Blue Helmets and unwilling to compromise their own national interests, the UN might soon lose its authority and thus its purpose.

2. Den Wortschatz erweitern und vertiefen – Globalisation

1

1 Making a mind map

With the list of terms below, make a mind map for the term *globalisation* in order to get a good idea of the different aspects.

First find the **five headings** under which the rest of the terms can be subcategorized. (Check them in the key before you take the next step.)

Then **add the terms to your headings**. Some terms may fall into more than one category. There will not be one perfect solution to this exercise; you might even want to introduce subcategories within the subcategories.

political system, trade, pollution, civil war, renewable energies, environment, religion, transport, treaty, living standards, Blue Helmets, outsourcing, UN, war, culture, ethnic issues, development, multinationals, fossil fuels, trade, conflicts, bilateral, values, internet, TV, global player, conflict, global warming, sanctions, natural resources, Security Council, communication, phones, satellites, technology transfer, multilateral, peace settlement, in/tolerance, General Assembly

2 Word families

Fill in the chart with the appropriate words.

nouns	verbs	adjectives
	to reinforce	
	to globalise	
benefit		
		provocative
settlement		
	to trade	—
negotiation		
		sanctioned
		intimidated; intimidating

3. Eine Prüfungsaufgabe bearbeiten – Analyse der Argumentationsstruktur

21 f. 89 1

The U.N. at 60 – What a disappointment!

by Daniel Mandel, Philadelphia Daily News, April 26, 2005

On April 26, 1945, diplomats convened in San Francisco to establish the United Nations. Sixty years later, it has never looked a bigger failure. Its founders would be amazed at the Frankenstein creation that now sits on Manhattan's East River.

The horrors of World War II had led statesmen from countries great and small to devise a council of nations to prevent the worst excesses of international conduct. An admirable ideal but it has not worked out that way.

Many blame the cold war for stunting the world body, but that confuses symptom with cause. With the anniversary and the raging debate about John Bolton's fitness to be U.N. ambassador, here are *some reasons* for the U.N. delinquency:

The General Assembly is not a democratic body.

Members represent not people, but governments, many squalid dictatorships. In U.S. terms, imagine a presidential ballot with every state represented by an equal number of electoral votes, and the voting in many states determined by cliques of gangsters, not the people, and the fraud on democracy is obvious.

The Security Council is beholden to the veto power of five very different permanent members.

Undoubtedly, this prevents the U.N. from doing much that's wicked but also most that's decent. The rare occasions on which the U.N. came to anyone's rescue – South Korea in 1950 and Kuwait in 1991 – were made possible by a Soviet boycott (never repeated) in one case and a rare abstention by China in the other.

Blocs of nations connive to render the U.N. impotent.

For example, no discussions are held, resolutions passed or action taken on China's obliteration of life and culture in Tibet.

For another, France, Russia and China were able for self-interested reasons to prevent the Security Council from enforcing its own resolutions on Iraq, leading the U.S. and its allies to do so on their own. A third: the 56-nation Organization of the Islamic Conference effectively vetoes any definition of terrorism that does not exempt the Palestinians.

Lack of democracy and human rights is no barrier to U.N. membership and participation.

Thus, its Human Rights Commission has lately included six of the world's most politically repressive regimes (Cuba, Saudi Arabia, Sudan, Libya, China, Vietnam) one of which (Libya) recently presided over it. The committee overseeing women's rights was recently headed by Iran, a country known for so-called "honor-killings" of wives and daughters. And while Saddam ruled in Baghdad, the committee on disarmament was presided over by Iraq.

And fatal structural flaws have rendered the U.N. ineffective and corrupt. Thus the oil-forfood scandal, providing humanitarian aid for Iraq degenerated into a network of graft that enriched Saddam and a host of middlemen, including U.N. officials. In the tsunami disaster, it was the U.S. and Australian navies that swiftly deployed forces to assist the millions of survivors. The best the U.N. could dispatch in that time were a group of concerned bureaucrats.

U.N. peace-keeping operations have also been conspicuously ineffective. Thus the disarming of Muslims in Srebrenica, leading to their slaughter and expulsion while their authorized protectors stood by. Or the enforced passivity of U.N. forces at the vital moment in Rwanda, permitting the massacre of up to 800,000 people, for which failure responsibility lies credibly at the door of the U. N. Secretary-General Kofi Annan.

[...] In short, there is little to celebrate 60 years on and even less reason to expect positive change. The U.S., which provides a quarter of the U.N. budget, should consider new ways to spend taxpayer money, holding the U.N. to performance standards before disbursing funds, backing a new caucus of democratic nations and reallocating funds to external initiatives that do some good, to name a few.

http://www.aijac.org.au/updates/Apr-05/280405.html#article_1 [08.04.10]

3 Analyse how the author's attitude is underlined by the composition of his article (Aufgabe 2: *analysis*).

The preparatory work has already been done.

Economic and Ecological Aspects in a Globalised World

1. Sich einen Überblick verschaffen

The **phenomenon of globalisation** is in fact nothing new. People have always **exchanged goods and ideas**. Oftentimes there is a **mutual benefit**, but just as often globalisation is set in motion by one side in a martial way and it is only that **one side that benefits**. This is also one of the most **controversial aspects** of our modern phase of globalisation: Is it really true that **everybody is likely to benefit from this process**?
When talking about globalisation, considering **economic consequences** for the individual or a certain country is one aspect; but this aspect is closely linked to another one that affects all of us everywhere: the **ecological consequences** of globalisation.

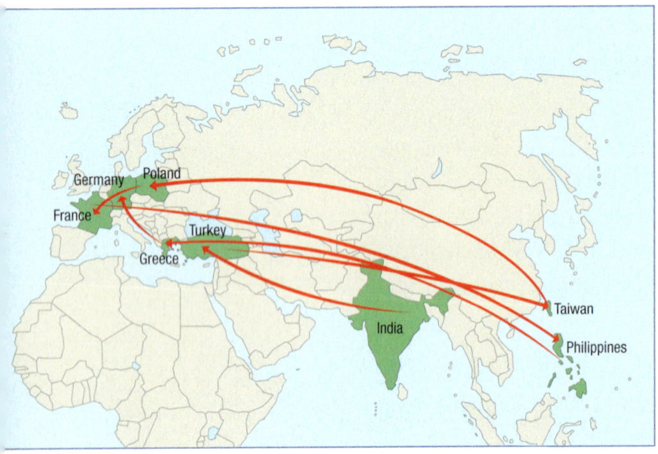

Transportation undergone during the production and distribution of jeans sold in Germany

As you can see from the map, a **pair of jeans often 'travels' over 30,000 miles** before they reach the consumer. Over 50 % of all jeans imported into Germany cost less than 10 Euros; this is so despite the fact that they are transported over thousands of kilometres. This **transport obviously causes a great deal of CO2 emission** which seems to be the **main factor of global warming** since the **burning of fossil fuels** (oil, coal and gas) by industrial estates, cars, ships and planes has been identified by many scientists as the primary reason for the increased emission of greenhouse gases. There are no incentives for companies to alter this production chain because their profits are maximised: The price of labour is extremely low because workers in developing countries work for very low wages in bad working conditions and there are no unions to interfere. At the same time, the **transportation costs are so low** that they hardly harm the profit margins. Obviously only **a few people** (namely cooperations and stockholders) profit from this absurd production line, but **many are harmed**: the workers in the developing countries because they are exploited to work under deplorable conditions; workers in developed countries because their jobs have been/will be moved to developing or take-off countries; everyone because the process of global warming is accelerated on a large scale.

There are of course skeptics who claim global warming – the warming process itself cannot be denied – is not anthropogenic, caused by human activity, but rather triggered by natural phenomena, e. g. increased solar activity and a higher frequency of volcanic eruptions. Nevertheless, temperature records show that the **ten warmest years since 1880**, when instrumental measurements began, all occurred **within the 12-year period of 1997–2008**.

Politicians especially from industrialised and take-off countries have been reluctant to sign treaties that would force them to dramatically cut their CO2 emissions because this would result in serious costs and possible setbacks to their economies. Therefore, the **internationally agreed upon goals for emission reduction and control have been very low** over the past decades and most countries have not even met those goals.

The effects of a **changing climate** are going to affect every region of our planet. Some areas will suffer extreme consequences such as **flooding or desertification**, while other regions will be less severely affected. Developing countries are more likely to be harmed not only due to their geographical location but also because they are less well-equipped to build means of protection, e.g. expensive levies.
But maybe **globalisation** can help us to solve problems, e.g. by **sharing knowledge, technologies and resources** in order to create a **cleaner global industry**, with economies that rely on **alternative and sustainable sources of energy** rather than on fossil fuels. Maybe we will succeed in building a world market with reasonable wages and working conditions for everyone, and thus a global market which does not profit from and harm the earth with unnecessary transport.

2. Wortschatz wiederholen und vertiefen – Economy and Ecology

2f.

1 Labelling pictures

Label this visual representation of global warming with the words given on the left.

The Greenhouse effect

oil and pertol engines; CFCs, aerosols; reflected radiation; radiation absorbed by greenhouse gases; deforestation; escaping radiation; absorbed by atmosphere and Earth; greenhouse gases and fossil fuels

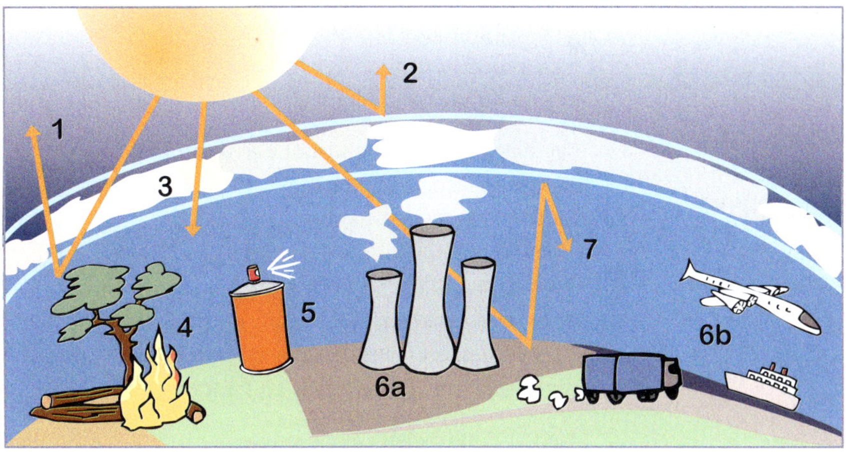

1. ______________ 2. ______________ 3. ______________

4. ______________ 5. ______________ 6a. ______________

6b. ______________ 7. ______________

2 Defining terms

Define the following three terms:

- developed or industrialised country
- developing country
- emerging or take-off country

3 Vocabulary in context

Using the following terms, **write a short text** in which you explain how consumers in an industrialised country may benefit from globalisation, whereas, at the same time, harm may be done to the economy of that country and to workers in developing or emerging countries.

to outsource production processes; minimum wage; maximise profits; unemployment; make redundant; sweatshops; unsafe workplace conditions; low environmental protection; no unions to protect workers' rights; economic dependencies on multinationals; hire-and-fire mentality

3. Eine Prüfungsaufgabe bearbeiten – Analyse einer Rede

ⓘ 22 f. ☑ 90 🔧 3 f.; 11

Obama's Speech on the Economy (January 8, 2009)

Throughout America's history, there have been some years that simply rolled into the next without much notice or fanfare, and then there are the years that come along once in a generation, the kind that mark a clean break from a troubled past and set a new course for our nation. This is one of those years.

We start 2009 in the midst of a crisis unlike any we have seen in our lifetime, a crisis that has only deepened over the last few weeks. Nearly 2 million jobs have been now lost, and on Friday we're likely to learn that we lost more jobs last year than at any time since World War II. Just in the past year, another 2.8 million Americans who want and need full-time work have had to settle for part time jobs. Manufacturing has hit a 28-year low. Many businesses cannot borrow or make payroll. Many families cannot pay their bills or their mortgage. Many workers are watching their life savings disappear. And many, many Americans are both anxious and uncertain of what the future will hold.

Now, I don't believe it's too late to change course, but it will be if we don't take dramatic action as soon as possible. If nothing is done, this recession could linger for years. The unemployment rate could reach double digits. Our economy could fall $ 1 trillion short of its full capacity, which translates into more than $ 12,000 in lost income for a family of four. We could lose a generation of potential and promise, as more young Americans are forced to forgo dreams of college or the chance to train for the jobs of the future. And our nation could lose the competitive edge that has served as a foundation for our strength and our standing in the world.

In short, a bad situation could become dramatically worse.

This crisis did not happen solely by some accident of history or normal turn of the business cycle, and we won't get out of it by simply waiting for a better day to come or relying on the worn-out dogmas of the past. We arrived at this point due to an era of profound irresponsibility that stretched from corporate boardrooms to the halls of power in Washington, D.C.

For years, too many Wall Street executives made imprudent and dangerous decisions, seeking profits with too little regard for risk, too little regulatory scrutiny, and too little accountability. Banks made loans without concern for whether borrowers could repay them, and some borrowers took advantage of cheap credit to take on debt they couldn't afford. Politicians spent taxpayer money without wisdom or discipline and too often focused on scoring political points instead of problems they were sent here to solve. The result has been a devastating loss of trust and confidence in our economy, our financial markets and our government.

Now, the very fact that this crisis is largely of our own making means that its not beyond our ability to solve. Our problems are rooted in past mistakes, not our capacity for future greatness. It will take time, perhaps many years, but we can rebuild that lost trust and confidence. We can restore opportunity and prosperity.

We should never forget that our workers are still more productive than any on Earth. Our universities are still the envy of the world. We are still home to the most brilliant minds, the most creative entrepreneurs and the most advanced technology and innovation that history has ever known. And we are still the nation that has overcome great fears and improbable odds.

If we act with the urgency and seriousness that this moment requires, I know that we can do it again. [...] For if we hope to end this crisis, we must end the culture of "anything goes" that helped create it. And this change must begin in Washington. It's time to trade old habits for a new spirit of responsibility. It is time to finally change the ways of Washington so that we can set a new and better course for America [...]

www.nytimes.com/2009/01/08/us/politics/08text-obama.html?_r=1 &pagewanted=print [08.03.10]

4 Analyse which rhetorical devices Barack Obama uses to convince his audience of his optimism (Aufgabe 2: *analysis*).

The rhetorical devices have already been underlined in different colours.

Science, Technology and Ethics in a Globalised World

1. Sich einen Überblick verschaffen

We live in an age of **rapid technological development**. Not only are we reaching out to the stars and sending machines on missions to far away planets, we are also permeating further and further into the smallest building blocks of life. Are we on the verge of finding solutions to everlasting youth, absolute health, even eternal life?

Listening to some scientists, one might think that thanks to **genetic engineering** we are indeed venturing into a bright future, into a brave new world. Some scientists offer to ensure that a couple's baby will not have the family's deadly hereditary disease, others promise to cure diseases such as Alzheimer or Parkinson. Some promise to feed the world with **genetically modified food** and thus put an end to starvation. Others want to prevent us from getting wrinkled and looking old. Others still want us to be able to colonise different planets when our planet Earth cannot accommodate us anymore. Yet others predict that we will soon merge with our technological inventions making them an integral part of our bodies, thus becoming powerful **cyborgs**.

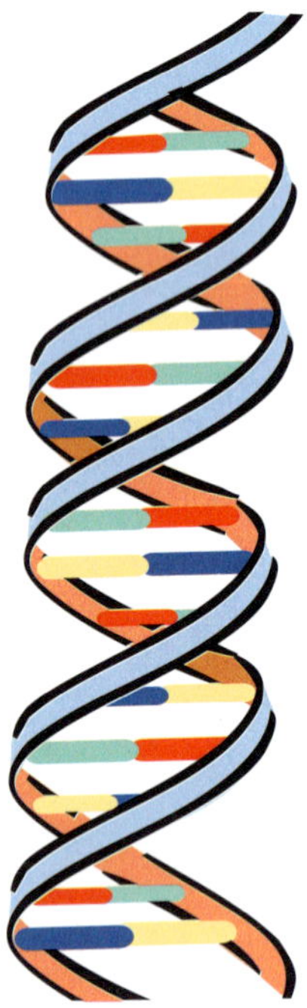

Whatever dreams scientists have been dreaming, there have always been voices who warned that these promises are **false promises**. Indeed, throughout history inventions heralded as a boon for mankind have turned out to be a curse after all, just as other inventions and findings have not turned out the curse they were made out to be. It is the duty not only of ethicists but also of scientists and every single individual to consider whether new scientific paths should be ventured on or are better left untaken.

Unfortunately, throughout history there has often been an **antagonism between scientists an ethicists**. At this stage in history, when we are able to destroy our planet and temper with the genetic codes of all creatures, it seems overdue for these classically opposing experts to finally work hand in hand: to ensure health and prosperity for all people and to avoid irrevocable catastrophes.

Up to now we can in no way heal an embryo of its diseases. What we can do is produce a considerable number of embryos, **screen** them, **select** the healthy ones and throw the sick ones away. One must consider whether this is not eugenics at a very early stage. Do we really want such a selection?

Genetically modified food, also known as **GM food**, is resistant to many natural hazards and thus seemingly better equipped to guarantee farmers their income and the rest of the people a stable supply of food. But so far the companies producing such seeds and animals make sure their products cannot reproduce naturally, thus ensuring that the farmers keep buying their seeds from them each season. It is useless to keep any grain from the last harvest since it is **infertile by design**. If the crop fails, and this has happened, the farmer is likely to go bankrupt and the food supply is in no way ensured, but rather largely endangered.

Many scientists fear that we will not perfect ourselves by integrating technologies into our bodies, but that **artificial intelligence** and thus computers and robots will surpass and eventually destroy or enslave humans. This **Point of Singularity**, as experts call the point at which artificial intelligence will outwit human intelligence, is estimated to occur within 20 to 40 years.

The challenges we are facing due to our fast-growing knowledge and rapid **technological advances** are enormous and so is the **responsibility** that comes with it. Such decisions as sketched above should not be made light-heartedly and the discussions should not be led in a contentious way – unfortunately they often are.

2. Wortschatz wiederholen und vertiefen – Genetic Engineering

4

1 Matching definitions and terms

Match the terms from the box below with the correct definitions.

a) ______________________ have the remarkable potential to develop into many different cell types in the body. Serving as a sort of repair system for the body, they can theoretically divide without limit to replenish other cells as long as the person or animal is still alive. Different types of these are: ______________________, ______________________, and __________________ *(start with the least and end with the most differentiated one)*.

b) ____________________ are composed of ____________________, a molecule in the shape of a double helix, a spiral ladder.

c) When male and female sex cells are brought together in a test tube in order to create a human embryo, this is called ____________________________.

d) There are three different types of cloning; they are sometimes mixed up:
____________________________ is the production of human embryos for use in research. The goal is to harvest stem cells that can be used to study human development and treat diseases. Stem cells are extracted from the egg after it has divided for 5 days. The extraction process destroys the embryo, which raises a variety of ethical concerns.

______________________________ is a technology used to generate an animal that has the same nuclear DNA as another currently or previously existing animal.

In ______________________________, genes from different organisms that improve taste and nutritional value or provide resistance to particular types of disease are used to produce genetically engineered crops.

e) ______________________________ is a method of identification often used in forensics. It compares fragments of DNA found within the cell nuclei of all living things. In mammals the strands of DNA are grouped into structures called chromosomes. With the exception of identical twins, the DNA of each individual is unique and can thus serve as means of identification.

f) ______________________________ uses a variety of laboratory techniques to determine whether a person has a genetic condition or disease or is likely to get the disease. Individuals may wish to know whether there is a family history of one specific disease, whether they show symptoms of a genetic disorder or whether it is likely that they will pass on a genetic problem to their children. Some employers and insurance companies would also like to use this but this has remained illegal so far.

g) The term ________________________ was first used in the 1950s and was originally used to describe the attempt to engineer ________________________ machines.

h) Scientists try to understand and simulate the brain's high-level ________________.

genetic testing, computational principles, DNA (deoxyribonucleic acid), reproductive cloning, DNA-cloning, stem cells, artificial intelligence, therapeutic cloning, intelligent, in vitro fertilisation, genetic fingerprinting, pluripotent, omnipotent, multipotent, genes

2 Prepositions

Fill in prepositions from the box below when necessary.

a) Scientists are interfering ____________________ the genetic code.

b) The impact ____________________ such research ________________ life in the future cannot be foreseen.

c) Some people might abuse ____________________ the knowledge.

d) It is essential to do further research ____________ the field of single-gene diseases.

e) Future generations will hold us accountable_________________ what we did or failed to do.

f) The reliability _________________ the genetic fingerprint has been the subject of controversial debates.

g) Children might have inherited a parent's resistance ___________ a certain disease.

h) There is a lot of distrust ________________ large agribusinesses.

I) There is a great fear _____________ society that robots will soon take _________.

j) So far human intelligence still reigns ________________ artificial intelligence.

within towards over (2x) for of (2x) in with to on

3. Eine Prüfungsaufgabe bearbeiten – Textzusammenfassung

16 f. 86 4 f.; 14

Why I still oppose GM crops

Verlyn Klinkenborg, guardian.co.uk, Tuesday 22 September 2009

For the past dozen years, I've been writing editorials opposing the introduction of genetically modified crops. When I began, genetically modified corn and soybeans were still just getting a foothold in American fields. Now, of course, hundreds of millions of acres here and abroad have been planted to these new varieties, which are usually engineered to withstand the application of pesticides – pesticides usually made by the same companies that engineer the seeds. Even wheat and rice producers, latecomers to the genetically modified table, are feeling the pressure to convert.

There has been a frenzy in the grain markets in the past couple of years – a new volatility in futures and in prices on the ground – that seems to favor genetically modified crops. It makes sense. The cost of conventionally-grown grain goes up and up because there is less and less of it. This leaves the world open to the nearly unchecked proliferation of genetically modified varieties.

After a dozen years, I still oppose genetically modified crops. This may sound like sheer truculence on my part – a Luddite reluctance to accept the future. It is certainly dispiriting. Like many people, I feel, as I did a decade ago, that genetically modified crops were introduced with bland assurances of safety based on studies from small test plots, a far different thing from the uncontrolled global experiment we now find ourselves in the midst of.

Scientists are still discovering the extent to which genetic fragments from these new crops can drift into other organisms. There is no evidence yet of catastrophic drift, where a genetic shard from a new crop cripples other organisms. But there is plenty of evidence to show that genetically modified fragments are turning up in places they're not wanted. The worry is not just how widespread the altered versions of familiar crops, like corn and soybeans, are becoming. It's also that many more conventional crops are being modified and that many more landscapes and ecosystems, yet untouched, will be planted with genetically modified varieties. [...]

But the trouble with genetically modified crops isn't merely the fact that they're genetically modified. It's that they embody so completely the troubling logic of modern agriculture. They demonstrate the tendency of commercial seeds to drive out traditional, locally adapted varieties, a pattern that has been intensifying since the introduction of hybrid corn in the 1930s. They exemplify the consistent bias toward expensive high-tech solutions, when, in much of the world, simple low-tech solutions still make much better, and much more affordable sense. They foster the spread of commodity crops, grown for cash, in place of subsistence crops.

Genetically modified crops create the illusion of more and better choices when, in fact, they represent a narrowing of genetic ownership and a model of genetic diversity that is unattainable outside the laboratory. Because of that, they may well turn out to decrease food security, especially as new non-food varieties – crops genetically modified to produce pharmaceuticals, for instance – go into production. The risk is enhanced by the licensing restrictions on genetically modified seeds that prevent independent research on their environmental impact. In effect, the GM seed industry is able to stifle research, even by agricultural scientists who are sympathetic to the technology.

Above all, genetically modified crops give the illusion of revolutionizing farming without actually changing much of anything. Farmers who plant them do spend less time – and less fuel – in the field, which is a good thing. But trying to pack a revolution into a seed won't do when the entire system needs revolutionizing. Industrial agriculture is antithetical to diversity of every kind – biological, social, cultural, political. To understand its real effects on diversity you have only to look at Brazilian soybeans, a commodity crop, growing where there was once Amazonian forest.

There is no disputing the enormous productivity of industrial agriculture, as long as you measure productivity solely in terms of the relationship between yield and labor and pay no attention to the health of the land or the well being of the people who live there. But in pursuing the unrelenting logic of an industrial version of agriculture we have left a world of alternatives unexplored.

The human species is still running ahead of the Malthusian prediction that we will outgrow our ability to feed ourselves. But this is a deeply troubling time for agriculture, as even a quick scan of the headlines reveals. Soaring food prices in the poorest parts of the world, soaring profits in the richest, ongoing – and wholly unnecessary – subsidies, growing competition between food and non-food crops, the list goes on and on.

To Americans, the continued resistance to genetically modified crops in other parts of the world may look Quixotic, a refusal to accept a done deal. But it is more than resistance to a type of seed. It is also resistance to a model of agriculture whose failings are all too plain.

3 Point out why the author is critical of GM crops. (Aufgabe 1: *comprehension*)

If you need help consult the notes below.

<u>Notes:</u>

- author <u>against</u> GM food (introduction; Autor, Ort und Zeit!!)
- CM corps dominate markets more and more → "enormous productivity", "farmers spend less time, less fuel" (pesticides?) → conventional crops become more expensive (2. Absatz)
- GM corps turn up on conventional crop fields → difficult to <u>not</u> become modified; no harm!?? to our bodies?? "uncontrolled global experiment" (3. Absatz)
- socio economic aspects: modern agriculture "bias towards high-tech solutions", "crops grown for cash" (rather than food! "subsistence crops" (5. Absatz)) → bad for poor countries, food more expensive (4. Absatz)
- ~~GM food lessens diversity in all aspects~~
- poor countries using GM crops → dependant on companies "genetic ownership" (4. Absatz)
- "soaring food prices" vs. "soaring profits" (4. Absatz)
- modern agriculture only focuses on profits not "health of the land" or "people who live there" (6. Absatz)

conclusion = <u>model has failed</u>

Utopian and Dystopian Worlds

1. Sich einen Überblick verschaffen

In 1516 Sir Thomas More published his novel *Utopia* and thus coined the term. Thomas More was by no means the first writer to imagine and reflect upon a perfect society which grants happiness and satisfaction to everyone, but the term **utopia** has since been used to describe such a society. The word itself is a neologism using Greek words: the prefix "eu" meaning either "good" or "no" and the noun "topos" meaning "place", thus combining the concept of a good or rather **ideal society that cannot really exist** anywhere. The term **dystopia** was derived much later as a contrast to utopia using "dys", the opposite of "eu", which marks something as bad or unfortunate. A **dystopia** is an imaginary **worst-case society**. Authors tend to take negative and **threatening tendencies** within their own society and **extrapolate** them, thus taking them to an extreme in order to illustrate the looming dangers in those trends.

Summing up one can say: In **utopian societies people's merits** and **most honourable character traits** are taken to the extreme, such as altruism, honesty, fairness, bravery, tolerance, modesty etc. In **dystopian societies people's vices** and **worst character traits** are taken to the extreme, such as greed, jealousy, ignorance, hypocrisy, intolerance etc.

Dystopian texts (e.g. novels, comics, films) mainly depict **two different types of dystopian societies**:

A dark and gloomy society often with an openly repressive government:
The vast majority of the citizens are suffering under the repressive system and/or under depressive and hostile circumstances. There is usually a small privileged elite who is in control. **Examples** of this type are *1984*, George Orwell (1948); *A Handmaid's Tale*, Margaret Atwood (1985); *Clockwork Orange*, Anthony Burgesse (1962); *The Wall*, Pink Floyd, Alan Parker (dir.) (1982); *Batman*, by artist Bob Kane and writer Bill Finger (1939).

A seemingly perfect society with seemingly happy and satisfied citizens:
A small, privileged elite **infringes freedom** and **enforces ignorance**. Real happiness and true emotions are often substituted by drug abuse and/or sex. **Examples** of this type are: *Fahrenheit 451*, Ray Bradbury (1953); *The Stepford Wives*, Ira Levin (1972); *The Matrix*, Wachowski brothers (wr. & dir.) (1999); *GATACCA*, Andrew Niccol (wr. & dir.) (1997); *In Blind Faith*, Ben Elton (2007).

Typical features characterising the societies in both types of dystopian texts are:

- **loss of freedom** (Thought Police, surveillance, iris scans, DNA tests)
- **loss of individuality** (cloning, overpopulation, no freedom of opinion, state or ideology is more important than the individual)
- **loss of true feelings** (friendship and privacy are infringed, separation of sex and love, drugs)
- **(mass) manipulation** (constant exposure to propaganda, no books, no art, entertainment instead of information)
- **total control** (constant surveillance through interactive screens, no free press, no rights, terror and torture)

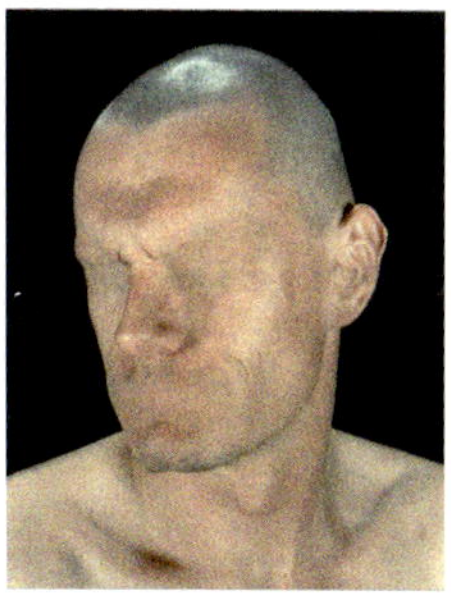

2. Wortschatz wiederholen und vertiefen – Dystopian Concepts

5

1 Adjectives and collocations -jumbled letters

Find the correct words. The letters in bold type indicate the correct first letter.

a) **d**cmotearic
toattilaarin → system
fastics

b) **s**upreepssvi
maelputivan → government
rsuselth

c) **r**sbeliuole
coouurages → hero
deeepstra

d) **t**rreoedisr
itngraon → public
tdferiire

2 Word families

Fill in the chart with the appropriate words.

nouns	verbs	adjectives
suppressor, suppression		
	to govern	
	—	ideological
propaganda		
		manipulative
		deceptive
	to distort facts	
		resistant
extrapolation		
	—	fundamentalist(-ic)

3. Eine Prüfungsaufgabe bearbeiten – Analyse des *settings*

31 f. 94 5 f.

Margret Atwood, *The Handmaid's Tale*, beginning of the second chapter

A chair, a table, a lamp. Above, on the white ceiling, a relief ornament in the shape of a wreath, and in the center of it a blank space, plastered over, like the place in a face where the eye has been taken out. There must have been a chandelier, once. They've removed anything you could tie a rope to. [...]

Think of it as being in the army, said Aunt Lydia. A bed. Single, mattress medium-hard, covered with a flocked white spread. Nothing takes place in the bed but sleep; or no sleep. I try not to think too much. Like other things now, thought must be rationed. There's a lot that doesn't bear thinking about. Thinking can hurt your chances, and I intend to last. I know why there is no glass, in front of the watercolor picture of blue irises, and why the window opens only partly and why the glass in it is shatterproof. It isn't running away they're afraid of. We wouldn't get far. It's those other escapes, the ones you can open in yourself, given a cutting edge.

So. Apart from these details, this could be a college guest room, for the less distinguished visitors; or a room in a rooming house, of former times, for ladies in reduced circumstances. That is what we are now. The circumstances have been reduced; for those of us who still have circumstances. But a chair, sunlight, flowers: these are not to be dismissed. I am alive, I live, I breathe. Where I am is not a prison but a privilege, as Aunt Lydia said.

Margret Atwood, *The Handmaid's Tale*, Fawcett Crest, New York, 1986, p. 9f.

Aldous Huxley, *Brave New World*, beginning of the first chapter

A squat grey building of only thirty-four stories. Over the main entrance the words, CENTRAL LONDON HATCHERY AND CONDITIONING CENTRE, and, in a shield, the World State's motto, COMMUNITY, IDENTITY, STABILITY.

The enormous room on the ground floor faced towards the north. Cold for all the summer beyond the panes, for all the tropical heat of the room itself, a harsh thin light glared through the windows, hungrily seeking some draped lay figure, some pallid shape of academic goose-flesh, but finding only the glass and nickel and bleakly shining porcelain of a laboratory. Wintriness responded to wintriness. The overalls of the workers were white, their hands gloved with a pale corpse-coloured rubber. The light was frozen, dead, a ghost. Only from the yellow barrels of the microscopes did it borrow a certain rich and living substance, lying along the polished tubes like butter, streak after luscious streak in long recession down the work tables.

"And this," said the Director opening the door, "is the Fertilizing Room."

Bent over their instruments, three hundred Fertilizers were plunged, as the Director of Hatcheries and Conditioning entered the room, in the scarcely breathing silence, the absentminded, soliloquizing hum or whistle, of absorbed concentration. A troop of newly arrived students, very young, pink and callow, followed nervously, rather abjectly, at the Director's heels. Each of them carried a notebook, in which, whenever the great man spoke, he desperately scribbled. Straight from the horse's mouth. It was a rare privilege. The D.h. C. for Central London always made a point of personally conducting his new students round the various departments.

Aldous Huxley, *Brave New World,* HarperCollins, New York, 2006

3 Illustrate how the authors establish the settings for their dystopian novels and compare the atmospheres that are thus created. (Aufgabe 2: *analysis*).

The American Dream Then and Now

1. Sich einen Überblick verschaffen

The term "American Dream" was coined by **James Truslow Adams** in his book *The Epic of America* (1931). He explains it as "that dream of a land in which life should be better and richer and fuller for everyone, with opportunity for each according to ability or achievement." In his definition we **find two cornerstones** of the American Dream: **equality** and **wealth**.

The **concept of equality** can be found in the cradle of the USA. What is now the USA started out as a British colony; like Australia it was a settlement colony, but unlike Australia the emigrants were not forced to leave Britain as convicts but rather went of their own free will **seeking religious or political freedom and fleeing persecution**. Thus, the idea of America as a place of greater freedom is a concept early engrained in its inhabitants; the so-called Pilgrim Fathers are an early symbol of this notion since they sailed to America in 1620 in order to seek religious freedom.

This concept was finally manifested in the **Declaration of Independence** (1776) in which it was explicitly stated that "**all men are created equal**, that they are endowed by their Creator with certain unalienable Rights, that among these are Life, Liberty and the pursuit of Happiness".

This **belief was already abandoned** during the westward expansion of the USA because these unalienable rights obviously did not **apply to Native Americans**. Neither did this claim refer to women, nor to Africans who were 'imported' and sold like goods and were merely regarded as property of their owners. **African-Americans** did not reach full and **equal civil rights until the early 1960s**. The whole concept of the **melting pot** did not seem to apply to them. Nowadays the concept of a **fruit salad** is often preferred as minorities wish to keep parts of their original identity, which they see as a positive contribution to America, just like a new fruit in a salad adds extra flavour to it.

Barack Obama seems to have **revived the American Dream** and is even regarded as **living proof** that it is still alive: He comes from a patchwork family of modest financial means and belongs to the African-American minority – nevertheless he has succeeded in becoming the **President of the USA**. This is what the American Dream is all about according to J. Truslow Adams: Everybody should be given the opportunity to fully develop according to their talents.

Today it is often claimed that the aspect of equality is neglected and that the **American Dream** has been **reduced to the aspect of wealth**, and thus reduced to the slogan 'from rags to riches'. The opportunity for everyone – regardless of class, ethnicity and origin – to be able to become rich has indeed always played an important role in the concept of what America is all about. In a society dedicated to capitalism, **the pursuit of happiness has become the pursuit of wealth**; success is solely measured by what you own, as many critics claim.

Nevertheless, the **appeal of the concept of equality and opportunity has not declined entirely**, as thousands attempt to immigrate to the USA legally or illegally each year. The American promise of freedom and wealth for everyone **still attracts people from all over the world** who are willing to leave everything behind in order to aspire to live their personal American Dream. On the pedestal of the Statue of Liberty, perhaps the best symbol of this American concept, we can read a sonnet which clearly alludes to both aspects:

"Give me your tired, your poor,
Your huddled masses yearning to breathe free,
The wretched refuse of your teeming shore.
Send these, the homeless, tempest-tost to me,
I lift my lamp beside the golden door!"
(Emma Lazarus, 1883)

Despite this noble claim, it must be acknowledged that not everyone who is poor and longing to breathe free is welcome in the USA. Immigration restrictions were already issued as early as the 19th century, e. g. during the Gold Rush in California in order to keep Chinese workers from becoming American citizens. Today very strict immigration laws and quotas are in place and the Mexican border is constantly being patrolled in order to capture and send back illegal immigrants, even though it is freely admitted that the Californian economy relies heavily on illegal workers.

2. Wortschatz wiederholen und vertiefen – Immigration

6 f.

1 Reasons for immigration, hopes and fears – an acrostic

Find suitable words.

S______ O______ L______

T______ F______ I______

A______ B______

T______ E______

U______ R______

E______ T______

Y______

2 Word square

Find 15 words connected with the topic of immigration. The words can be hidden vertically, diagonally and horizontally.

R	E	F	U	G	E	E	C	O	L	P	J	H	T	V	B	P	O	R
T	Z	A	S	S	T	A	N	C	E	S	T	O	R	L	O	E	N	N
W	E	S	T	I	L	O	S	F	T	U	O	L	N	J	K	N	O	I
X	U	I	O	U	D	H	G	W	P	U	R	S	U	I	T	N	T	S
E	U	P	O	P	G	I	S	S	E	T	R	O	G	T	A	I	L	O
N	U	O	L	R	M	M	S	G	R	A	D	S	E	R	T	L	L	L
O	H	G	H	O	O	L	T	C	Q	U	T	I	N	P	O	E	T	A
P	Z	O	O	O	T	J	L	N	R	U	I	S	G	H	T	S	M	T
H	E	R	S	T	L	O	I	M	N	I	D	R	H	U	I	S	B	I
O	B	O	T	E	H	L	X	E	R	N	M	W	O	O	C	H	L	O
B	R	I	I	D	E	P	R	E	J	U	D	I	C	E	P	O	O	N
I	T	L	L	G	E	T	R	A	M	L	O	N	N	S	T	R	O	P
A	T	A	I	G	E	R	U	T	S	O	L	L	A	A	M	O	L	N
Q	O	L	T	U	T	R	M	P	O	P	O	V	E	R	T	Y	G	L
U	L	O	Y	H	F	G	T	O	O	U	R	T	L	M	W	I	O	O
M	A	N	G	O	S	T	I	N	E	R	T	A	S	T	R	E	O	G
M	E	L	T	I	N	G	P	O	T	P	U	O	L	P	O	S	T	N
R	O	I	T	D	E	P	R	I	V	E	D	O	P	P	O	L	O	G
P	U	Z	R	U	N	D	E	R	P	R	I	V	I	L	E	G	E	D

3. Eine Prüfungsaufgabe bearbeiten – Charakterisierung

34 f. 96 7 f.

The following text is an extract from the drama *Death of a Salesman* by *Arthur Miller*. It is about Will Loman, an unsuccessful businessman who is married with two sons, Biff and Happy. Biff is two years older than his brother.

Biff: Well, I spent six or seven years after high school trying to work myself up. Shipping clerk, salesman, business of one kind or another. And it's a measly manner of existence.To get on that subway on the hot mornings in summer. To devote your whole life to keeping stock, or making phone calls, or selling or buying. To suffer fifty weeks of the year for the sake of a two-week vacation, when all you really desire is to be outdoors, with your shirt off. And always to have to get ahead of the next fella. And still – that's how you build a future.

Happy: Well, you really enjoy it on a farm? Are you content out there?

Biff [*with rising agitation*]: Hap, I've had twenty or thirty different kinds of job since I left home before the war, and it always turns out the same. I just realized it lately. In Nebraska when I herded cattle, and the Dakotas, and Arizona, and now in Texas. It's why I came home now, I guess, because I realized it. This farm I work on, it's spring there now, see? And they've got about fifteen new colts. There's nothing more inspiring or

– beautiful than the sight of a mare and a new colt. And it's cool there now, see? Texas is cool now, and it's spring. And whenever spring comes to where I am, I suddenly get the feeling, my God. I'm not gettin' anywhere. What the hell am I doing, playing around with horses, twenty-eight dollars a week! I'm thirty-four years old, I oughta be makin' my future. That's when I come running home. And now, I get here, and I don't know what to do with myself. [After a pause] I've always made a point of not wasting my life, and everytime I come back here I know that all I've done is to waste my life.

Happy: You're a poet, you know that, Biff? You're a – you're an idealist!

Biff: No, I'm mixed up very bad. Maybe I oughta get married. Maybe I oughta get stuck into something. Maybe that's my trouble. I'm like a boy. I'm not married, I'm not in business, I just – I'm like a boy. Are you content, Hap? You're a success, aren't you? Are you content?

Happy: Hell, no!

Biff: Why? You're making money, aren't you?

Happy [*moving about with energy, expressiveness*]: All I can do now is wait for the merchandise manager to die. And suppose I get to be merchandise manager? He's a good friend of mine, and he just built a terrific estate on Long Island. And he lived there about two months and sold it, and now he's building another one. He can't enjoy it once it's finished. And I know that's just what I would do. I don't know what the hell I'm workin' for. Sometimes I sit in my apartment – all alone. And I think of the rent I'm paying. And it's crazy. But then, it's what I always wanted. My own apartment, a car, and plenty of women. And still, goddammit, I'm lonely.

Biff [*with enthusiasm*]: Listen, why don't you come out West with me?

Happy: You and I, heh?

Biff: Sure, maybe we could buy a ranch. Raise cattle, use our muscles. Men built like we are should be working out in the open.

Happy [*avidly*]: The Loman Brothers, heh?

Biff [*with vast affection*]: Sure, we'd be known all over the counties!

Happy [*enthralled*]: That's what I dream about, Biff.

Extract from: Arthur Miller, Death of a Salesman, Act 1, London, Penguin, 2000, Reprinted by Permission of International Creative Management Inc. © 1949, 1977 by Arthur Miller, pp. 16 ff.

3 Analyse the two characters. In what way do the two brothers represent the *American Dream*? (Aufgabe 2: *analysis*)

If you need help consult the German *Erwartungshorizont* below.

Biff repräsentiert die Lebenshaltung des „Go West!" der Pioniere. Er hat bisher seine Ungebundenheit und Freiheit in der Natur („all you really desire is to be outdoors, with your shirt off", Z. 5 f.) genossen und den Idealen der gutbürgerlichen Welt den Rücken gekehrt („Maybe I oughta get stuck into something. Maybe that's my trouble. I'm like a boy. I'm not married. I'm not in business …", Z. 22–24). Ideale: Ungebundenheit; Teil der Natur sein; Abenteuerlust, etc.
Im Unterschied dazu repräsentiert **Happy** das amerikanische Ideal eines Menschen, der es durch Arbeit zu etwas gebracht hat. Erfolg in diesem Sinne bedeutet, eine gute berufliche Position, eine Wohnung und ein Auto zu haben (vgl. Z. 28 f.; 34 f.). Nur den Wunsch nach einer Familie hat er sich noch nicht erfüllen können (vgl. Z. 35). Ideale: sich hocharbeiten; Sicherheit; Potenziale ausschöpfen etc.
In beiden Biographien zeigen sich jedoch gleichzeitig auch die Grenzen des *American Dream*. Beide Brüder sind unzufrieden mit ihrem Leben, da sie ihren Lebenssinn nicht gefunden haben.

Postcolonial Encounters

1. Sich einen Überblick verschaffen

A very brief timeline of Britain's colonial history

1588 Under the reign of Queen Elisabeth I, the Spanish Armada is defeated. → British dominance at sea

This 1796 painting by Philippe-Jacques de Loutherbourg depicts the English victory over the Spanish Armada in the battle of Gravelines.

1601 Ireland under English rule.

1770 James Cook discovers the eastern coast of Australia and claims the continent for Britain.

Replica of Cook's ship the "Endeavour" in Cooktown harbour

1776 The United States of America declare their independence from Great Britain and the English King.

Declaration of Independence, by John Trumbull, 1756–1843

1867 Canada becomes the first independent Dominion, other settlement colonies soon follow (last one: South Africa 1910).

Canadian flag used 1868–1921

1890s

Cecil Rhodes, pioneer of British expansion in Africa, suggests a "Cape to Cairo" railway linking the strategically important Suez Canal to the mineral-rich South. The project was never realised.

Caricature of Cecil John Rhodes in Punch 1892

1920s

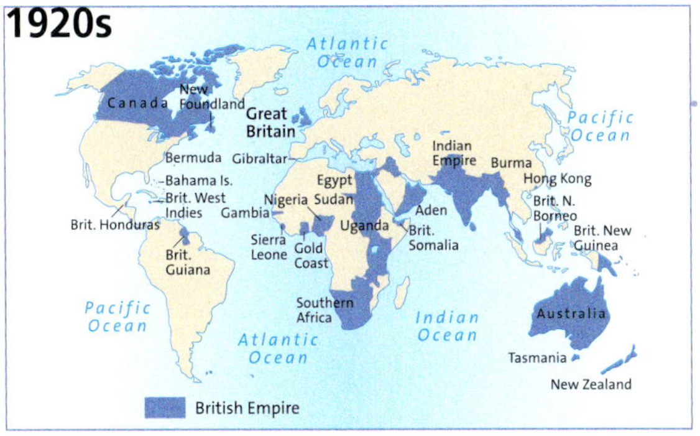

The British Empire covers 35 % of the world's land area and rules over 25 % of the world's population.

1945

The end of World War II marks the beginning of the decay of the Empire which is slowly transformed into the Commonwealth.

Freedom At Midnight: 1947, India, Pandit Jawaharlal Nehru being sworn in as Prime Minister

1949

The Commonwealth symbol

The new Commonwealth is founded as an institution of freely and equally associated states. Most former colonies become part of this newly founded political body.

The **Commonwealth** defines itself as an "association of sovereign nations that support each other and work together towards international goals". Nevertheless, there are many people who are dissatisfied with how the past is dealt with, and that it is not acknowledged that the Commonwealth is really just all the countries Britain used to own. Many people in Commonwealth countries other than Great Britain think that contemporary notions of the Commonwealth often ignore the day-to-day **horrors associated with the Empire and colonisation**. Many claim that the consequences of colonialism, exploitation and racism are still felt today in the former colonies.

Others still hold up the old **imperial credo** that Britain and its '**benefits of civilisation**', such as railroads, educational and health systems, enriched those countries and therefore helped them to get a better start into independence. Yet others agree that although colonialism was a horrifying experience for the colonised nations, they should be able to get their act together now after **50 years of independence** and colonialism cannot be blamed for today's problems.

2. Wortschatz wiederholen und vertiefen – British Colonialism

8

1 Vocabulary in context

Fill in the gaps with the appropriate words. Compare introductory text

It can be argued that Great B_ _ _ _ _ _'_[1] ascent to a superpower started with the d_ _ _ _ _[2] of the Spanish Ar_ _ _ _[3] in 1588 which established it as a major na_ _ _[4] power. English captains sailed all around the gl_ _ _[5] discovering and taking possession of new ter_ _ _ _ _ _ _ _[6] for the English Crown. The fou_ _ _ _ _[7] of Virginia was soon followed by the es_ _ _ _ _ _ _ _ _ _ _ _[8] of more British c_ _ _ _ _ _ _[9] along the North American coast.

While the loss of the North American colonies – except Ca_ _ _ _[10] – in 1776 marked a severe defeat for the British E_ _ _ _ _ _[11] it was also during this period that other territories were dis_ _ _ _ _ _ _[12] and thus compen_ _ _ _ _[13] for the losses in America: Australia (1770), the Cape Colony (1814) and later New Zealand (1841) were – like the lost American colonies – regarded as settl_ _ _ _ _[14] colonies (although Australia started out with con_ _ _ _ _[15]).

Furthermore, Britain exp_ _ _ _ _[16] its influence in Asia, particularly in In_ _ _[17] which was to become its most valuable colony.

It was under the re_ _ _[18] of Queen Victoria (1837 – 1901) that the British Empire experienced its greatest exp_ _ _ _ _ _ _[19]; further territories especially on the A_ _ _ _ _ _[20] continent were added during this period. With the opening of the Su_ _[21] Canal in 1867, trade with the So_ _ _[22] East A_ _ _ _[23] colonies in general and India in particular was facilitated a great deal which made those t_ _ _ _[24] routes even more profi_ _ _ _ _[25]. The importance of this waterway and that of Gib_ _ _ _ _ _ _[26] cannot be underestimated and is the reason why Britain has always been particularly eager to en_ _ _ _[27] its control over them. Gib_ _ _ _ _ _ _[28] still belongs to Great Britain to this very day (since 1704) even though Spain, also a me_ _ _ _[29] of the EU, has been recl_ _ _ _ _ _[30] it for decades.

By 1921, after former Ger_ _ _[31] colonies had been handed over to the winners of WW I, the British Empire ru_ _ _[32] 35 % of the world's land area and 25 % of the world's population were the su_ _ _ _ _ _[33] of King George V.

3. Eine Prüfungsaufgabe bearbeiten – kreativer Schreibauftrag

35 f. 97 8; 9

A.T. Nwaubani is a graduate of Psychology from the University of Ibadan, Nigeria. She made her very first income from winning a writing competition at the age of thirteen. She's based in Abuja, Nigeria, and has just accepted an offer from Hyperion Books US to publish her first novel.

Adaobi Tricia Nwaubani, Coming to the UK

Somebody stomped on my foot while another person dragged at the collar of my brand new polyester shirt. I felt my feet being hoisted off the ground; my face became trapped in a damp, bristly female armpit. Nevertheless, I pressed on through the horde of morning breath and adrenaline-soaked sweat without stopping. All of us had one common goal. Everybody wanted to be first to cross the partly-opened gates.

'Behave yourselves, behave yourselves!' the potbellied security man howled. But the gusto on his face did not correspond with the rage in his voice. He was living the plebeian's dream—the opportunity to exercise some morsel of tyranny. 'You people shouldn't annoy me this morning!' he continued, howling even louder than before.

The crowd paid no attention to him and continued surging forward like a plague of rats being lured by the Pied Piper of Hamelin's tune. Seeing their high commander so defiantly ignored, the more gaunt security men descended on the crowd with curses and whips. Yelps of pain sprang up from the crowd in rapid intervals, like firecrackers on a New Year's Eve. Half-heartedly, we attempted to restore what had just a few seconds ago, been an orderly queue. A few clever ones exploited the commotion as the perfect opportunity for them to steal a place or two ahead of their original positions.

[...] at noon, the gates to the British High Commission compound had been thrown open to allow us into the visa-processing section of the building.

When it got to my turn, the lady behind the counter stared indifferently and rattled something I did not understand. 'Black-British', I learnt people like her were called these days.

'Pardon?' I asked, venturing an imitation of her nasal accent.

'That would be seven thousand naira,' she clarified sternly, like a female post office clerk.

Reluctantly, my fingers parted with the bundle of crisp five-hundred naira notes which I had secured in my knee-length socks while hustling my way into the building. All my labours of the past few hours would have been thoroughly wasted if I did not have the fee in advance. I received a numbered ticket in exchange for the cash and headed for one of the bleak wooden benches that lined the large hall.

'Phew,' I sighed.

It was a relief to be finally resting my feet on solid ground and breathing in some organized air. Technically, I was even now on British soil. Despite the fact that there was neither wintry breeze nor freezing rain on this December morning, the Embassy grounds was the United Kingdom itself. Or at least, that is what the governments of this world had agreed to have everybody believe. I stretched out my feet beneath the bench in front of me and relaxed. Then I focused my thoughts on the chief issue at hand.

The chances of my UK visa being approved were low—very low. To be honest, few visa-processing officers in their right minds would accept that a young, jobless man with no strong family ties in Nigeria was simply travelling to London on holiday; but it was worth giving it a try as so many others before me had done. [...]

My meditations were interrupted by a dull thud on my right. I turned and saw a dense crop of jerry-curled hair belonging to a short, thickset man who had just landed in the seat right next to me. The man adjusted his bulky frame on the plywood and sat straight. He was wearing a Burberry jacket, a Burberry pair of trainers, and had a Hugo Boss pair of sunglasses hooked into the front of his Tommy Hilfiger t-shirt. I recognized him as one of the exuberant troublemakers who had irked the waiting crowd outside. He had tried to wangle his way closer to the front of the queue even before the gates were thrown open. Hmm. How had he made it into the hall so quickly? The man swivelled his head suddenly. I did not divert my eyes quickly enough. His eyes caught mine and held onto them very tightly. Then he grinned and stretched out an arm, 'My brother, what's up? How are things?' [...]

www.african-writing.com/nwaubani.htm [08.03.10]

2 Continue the story: What might happen to the narrator now that he has made it into the visa-processing section of the British embassy? Will the arrival of the "exuberant troublemaker[s]" (l. 44) have any effect?
(Aufgabe 3: *evaluation: re-creation of text*)

Before you start writing, consider the following aspects. Tick the aspects that are fitting for the story and **make sure you use them accordingly in your own text**.

Why is the narrator at the British embassy?	☐ He wants to apply for a job at the embassy. ☐ He wants to apply for a tourist visa. ☐ He wants to apply for a business visa.
Point of view, narrative perspective	☐ first person ☐ third person limited ☐ omniscient
Tone/mood	☐ tense and fearful ☐ dark and moody ☐ funny and ironic ☐ sarcastic and bitter
Language, register	☐ casual, colloquial ☐ sophisticated ☐ limited
Attitude towards the British High Commission	☐ submissive ☐ ambiguous ☐ fearful
How will the "exuberant troublemaker[s]" affect the narrator's application?	...

Cross Cultural Experiences

1. Sich einen Überblick verschaffen

According to the chart below, there is a greater proportion of non-European citizens in Great Britain than in Germany. This is mainly due to the fact that **Great Britain** was, for many centuries, the **leading colonial and thus world power** while Germany had far less worldwide influence. During the process of **decolonisation** in the last century, many people from these former colonies have left their home countries and immigrated to Great Britain. This has made Great Britain an extremely **diverse and multicultural place** with people whose roots are from Asia, Africa as well as the Caribbean.

	Great Britain	Germany
Total population	100 % (58,789,194)	100 % (82,501,000)
Caucasian/White	92.1 %	96.27 % (+ Turkey 98.4 %)
Non-European	7.9 %	1.6 % (+ Turkey 3.73 %)
Asian	4 %	1.0 % (+ Turkey 3.1 %)
African	0.8 % (Black African)	0.34 %

Data: Statistisches Bundesamt Deutschland 2005; www.statistics.gov.uk

The influx of so many people with different cultural, social and religious backgrounds has been leaving its **imprint on British society**: Multiculturalism has caused a **considerable dynamic and vitality** in Britain's **cultural life** but also in its **economy**: Many festivals from all over the world have become an integral part of the British calendar and are an excellent opportunity for the people of a community to get together and meet one another; they learn about traditions, customs and enjoy 'exotic' food which has definitely enriched British cuisine. In addition, there are the close links that many immigrants still have to their home countries which have been a great advantage in a globalised world and have given Great Britain a head start in many fast-growing economies such as India.

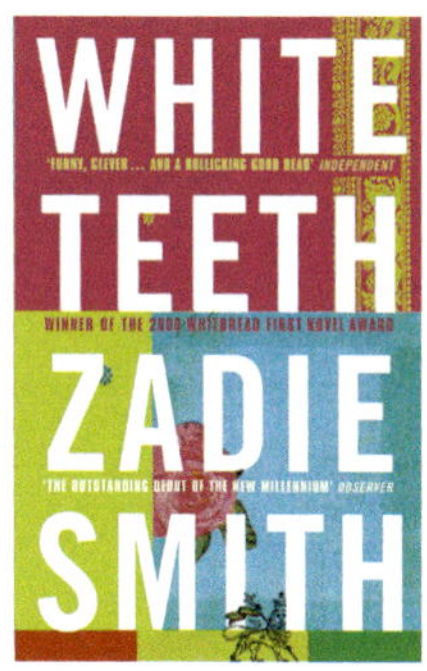

There have, of course, also been **problems caused by immigration**. Integration is still a touchy subject and an unsolved problem. Some people think that 7.9 % non-European citizens is just too much and this endangers British **identity**. How much should an immigrant or a British citizen of foreign background (e. g. second- or even third-generation immigrants) assimilate? Can the majority expect any adaptation at all in a free and democratic state? Unfortunately, the attacks of September 11th in New York and terror attacks in London have fuelled a growing suspicion towards Muslim citizens and immigrants; some people even claim that **Islamaphobia** is on the rise.

As the social strata within the **ethnic minorities** is changing, the questions mentioned above are increasingly being taken up and discussed by the minorities themselves. This has been reflected in a large and successful output of movies, plays, novels, etc.

2. Wortschatz wiederholen und vertiefen – Multiculturalism

9

1 A crossword puzzle

Compare introductory text

ACROSS
1) process of coming to live permanently in a country
7) opposite of minority
9) to increase
11) celebration
13) country that is ruled by another country
16) not part of Europe (adj.)
17) process of mixing people from different backgrounds

DOWN
2) lasting effect
3) relationship between production, trade and money
4) to improve
5) habit or ritual typical of a particular culture
6) blending of minorities into a dominant society
8) to put people into a situation where they could be harmed
10) the co-existence of various cultures in one society
12) belonging to a country that controls another country (adj.)
14) the sum of characteristics that distinguish people from others
15) all people living in a particular area

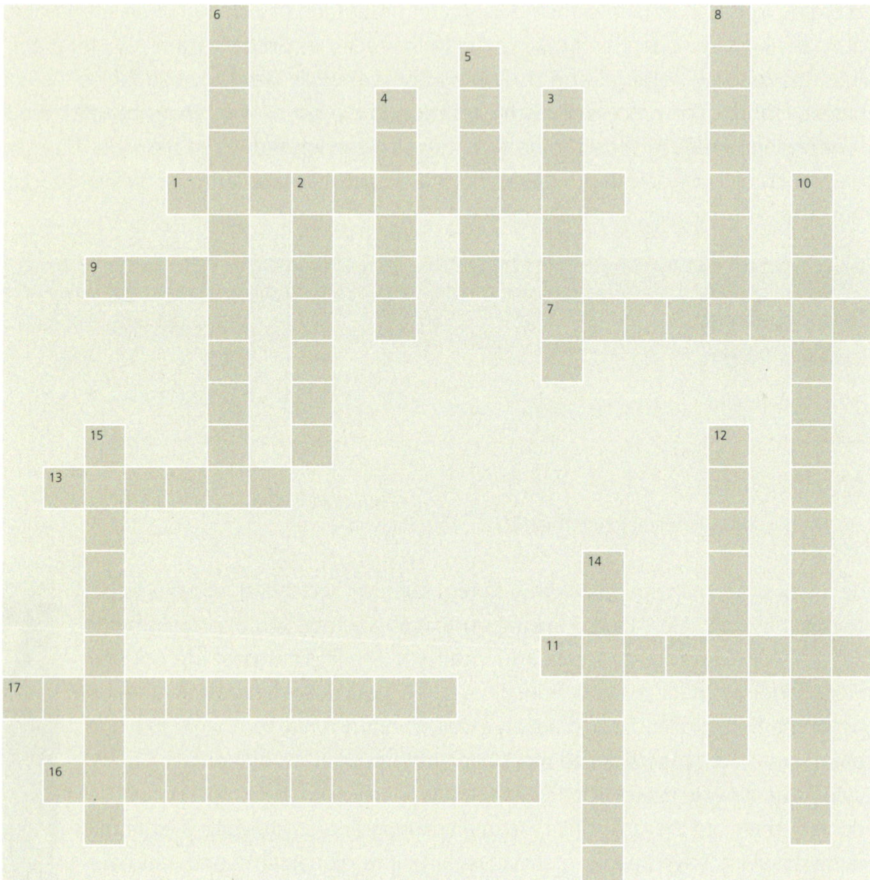

3. Eine Prüfungsaufgabe bearbeiten – Analyse der Erzählperspektive und eines *stills;* kreativer Schreibauftrag

32; 35; 39 | 95; 97; 99 | 9 f.

After an arranged marriage, Nazneen, the protagonist of this novel, has to move from Bangladesh to London to live with her husband Chanu, also a Bangladeshi, who is twenty years older. The couple has two daughters – but overall the family is not happy: Nazneen starts a secret affair with a man her own age, Chanu cannot live up to his professional aspirations and the girls reject their Muslim background – they want to be as British as possible. Chanu eventually decides, that he wants to move back to Bangladesh, a night-mare not only for his daughters, but also for his wife. Despite their opposition, Chanu, as head of the family, is determined to ensure that they all move back. He has already bought plane tickets and everything is packed when he realises that neither his wife nor his daughters are willing to follow him. In the excerpt given here, he announces his decision to go to Bangladesh alone, leaving his family behind in London.

Chanu had called his daughters. "There has been a change of plan." He rubbed his face with his palms, getting the blood to flow again. "I have suggested, and your mother has agreed, that the three of you come later." He weighed his stomach and slapped it around a little. He cleared his throat and this time the obstruction seemed genuine; it brought tears to his eyes. "I'll go on ahead now, clear—ahem—the path."

The girls looked at Nazneen. They saw that it was true. Bibi chewed the ends of both her plaits. Shahana went to her father and put her arms around his neck. "But who will cook for you, Abba?"

"Who will cut your corns?" said Bibi.

Chanu tickled Shahana under the arms. "What? Do you not know? I am a better cook than your mother. And look, Bibi, my stomach has gone flatter than a paratha. I can reach my own toes now." He bent down to prove it. Then he began to rearrange bags and money, tickets and passports. He clicked on his money belt and tested the catch. "Be good girls, do as your mother tells you, finish your homework every night, don't waste time on television and all that rubbish, read Tagore (I recommend Gitanjali), don't think that there's anything you're not good enough for, remember that—" He broke off. "Yes, well. That should do for now."

Extract from: Monica Ali, *Brick Lane*, Random House, New York, 2003, p. 526.

2 Analyse the point of view in the text extract. Then analyse the still and explain how it mirrors the narrative perspective from the text and how it differs, consider different aspects of camera work. (Frage 2: *analysis*)

3 Rewrite this excerpt from Chanu's point of view. (Frage 3: *evaluation: re-creation of text*)

Great Britain's Way into the EU

1. Sich einen Überblick verschaffen

Since the decline of the Empire after WW II **Great Britain** has been **torn betwee**n its loyalties and its political and economic interests, leaning either towards the **Commonwealth of Nations** or the **EU**. The latter is ever increasing in power and importance while the former hardly carries any political power and cannot match the EU's economic wealth. Britain joined the then so-called EEC in 1963.

One key factor why the **EU** has become **more powerful** over the last decades is the fact that the member states have worked towards a **single market**, even introducing a **single currency** in 1999 which has dramatically **facilitated trade** and has given a boost to many national economies within the EU. The crucial steps towards these changes were taken in 1987, when the Single European Act was signed, mapping out a route towards a free-flow of trade across the EU; and in 1991 the Maastricht Treaty established the time schedule towards a single European currency, the Euro. **Great Britain** and a few other members of the EU, as you can see in the map below, did **not give up their national currencies**.

Those economic decisions which have helped to make the EU a strong international marketplace are precisely the factors which **eurosceptics** – not only found in Britain – **fear**, since they imply that member states alter national laws in order to confirm to the new European laws and ways of trading. The price for this economic boost has indeed been a **loss of national power**, which is most apparent in the vanishing of national currencies like the Deutsch-Mark, Pesos, Kronen, etc.

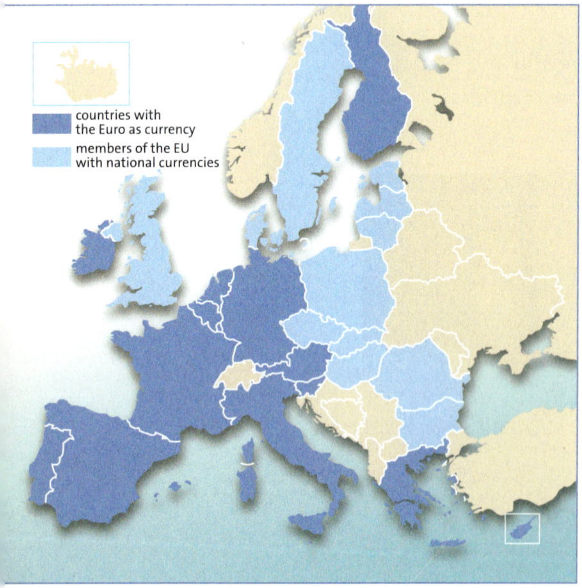

But not only economic doubts fuel British scepticism. Many **British** are proud of their **long and stable democratic heritage** – to be traced back as far as 1215 when the Magna Carta was signed – which had been established long before other European nations embraced the concept of democracy. British eurosceptics are afraid that by giving up too many rights to the lawmakers in Brussels, they are eventually going to **lose their sovereignty, their long standing institutions and their traditions**. Many are eager to protect these traditions against the infiltration of the EU which is widely associated with a lack of democracy and a lot of red tape.

Even though the EU does not seem to be very popular with the majority of the British population, British governments in the past decades have stressed the importance of the EU for Great Britain and have clearly stated that Great Britain is very much a crucial part of the EU. Therefore, the **British government has strongly supported the Lisbon Treaty**; both Houses of Parliament have debated the Treaty and eventually voted strongly in favour of it.

2. Wortschatz wiederholen und vertiefen – The European Union

10

1 Find the synonyms.

You can find the solutions in the introductory text.

a) to discuss –
b) to disappear –
c) to be in favour of –
d) to show –
e) independence –
f) richness –
g) to defend/shelter –
h) too much bureaucracy –
i) influence –
j) decrease –
k) contract –
l) to change –
m) tradition –

2 Find opposites.

You can find the solutions in the introductory text.

a) to complicate –
b) against –
c) supporters –
d) decrease –
e) benefit –
f) minority –
g) dynamic –
h) to keep –
i) to detest –
j) weak –

3 Complete the terms indicating key factors of the European Union:

You can find the solutions in the introductory text.

a) **s**__________ **m**__________

b) **s**__________ **c**__________

c) **to fa**__________ **t**__________

d) **l**__________ **of n**__________ **p**__________

e) **E**__________ **l**__________

3. Eine Prüfungsaufgabe bearbeiten – Analyse und Vergleich von Text und Bild; Schreiben eines Leserbriefs

19; 27 f. 88; 92 11; 12

WHY SHALLOW BLAIR MUST NOT LORD IT OVER US ALL AGAIN

By Leo McKinstry, Monday, October 5th 2009, Daily Express

THE EU juggernaut grinds on remorselessly, crushing the last gasps of independence from the member nations. Now that the people of Ireland have been bullied and brainwashed into voting for the Lisbon Treaty, the Euro-fanatics' plans for a united superstate can be fully enacted.

The centrepiece of this drive for European political unity is the creation of a new post of EU president. As if the destruction of our national freedoms were not depressing enough, it is clear that the overwhelming favourite for the presidency is none other than Tony Blair, our shallow, discredited former Prime Minister.

Having wrecked our country once with his destructive brand of messianic socialism, now he wants to come back for another go. According to one EU official, Blair could be provisionally appointed to the job before the end of October. His wife Cherie, notorious for her grasping behaviour, may already be eyeing up multi-million-pound properties in Brussels.

But it would be an outrage if Blair was foisted on us as EU President. Such a move would make a mockery of democracy, for he would have not the slightest mandate to govern us. For a start, the British people have never been allowed to vote on the establishment of the EU Presidency, the Labour Government having reneged on its promise to hold a referendum on the new treaty.

Just as importantly, Blair will be able to take power without having been voted into office by any of the electorates of Europe since, as in the old Soviet Union, the President will be appointed by the EU's ruling council. The European Union's bosses are fond of lecturing the rest of the world about the importance of democracy but their spectacular elitism means that they never apply such principles to their own closed, unaccountable regime.

The idea of an unelected President Blair is enough to provoke thoughts of revolution. In the past, we were always able to throw out our rulers if they became too arrogant or incompetent but that becomes an impossibility in the new Europe created by Lisbon. Without the safety valve of the ballot box, we are stuck with this grinning, patronising, war-mongering socialist, whom most of us were sick of years ago. [...]

Hugh Gaitskell, one of Blair's predecessors as Labour leader, said in 1962 that European integration would mean "the end of a thousand years of history" of British independence. The presidency of Tony Blair could mark the final page in that glorious, but fading history.

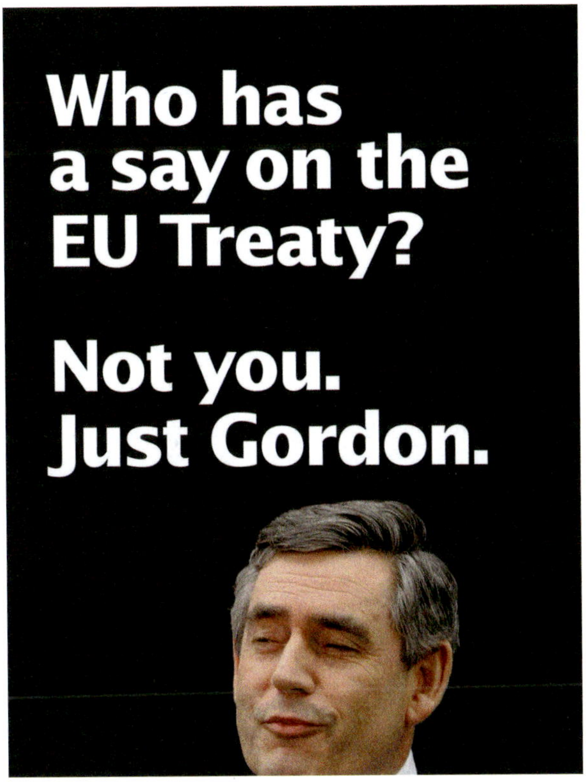

Annotation: Gordon Brown – successor of Tony Blair as (Labour) Prime Minister of Great Britain

4 Compare the attitudes towards the EU and in particular the Lisbon Treaty revealed in the text and on the poster; examine how the reader is influenced to share the points of view presented. (Aufgabe 2: *analysis*)

If you need help, have a look at the words and phrases below.

text: EU = threat to freedom, absence of democratic legitimacy, hypocritical, marks end of Britain's independence
polemic, personal attacks, Blair as incarnation of all evils of the EU, choice of words, comparison to the undemocratic system of the Soviet Union, insinuation of helplessness

picture: EU = arrogant and threatening, lack of democracy
arrogant look, rhetorical question, sarcasm, colour black, Brown as personification of EU's and Britain's lack of democracy

5 Write a letter to the editor in which you comment on the article by Mr. McKinstry. Refer to content and form. (Aufgabe 3: *evaluation: re-creation of text*)

Shakespeare – the Great Bard

1. Sich einen Überblick verschaffen

His Age – The Elizabethan or the Golden Age
For information on this topic check out the vocabulary exercise no. 1.

His Theatre – The Globe Theatre in Southwark, London
During the Elizabethan Age **theatres were extremely popular** and profitable. The Globe, built in 1597–1598, could accommodate up to 3000 people and because people did not want to see a piece twice, **playwrights** were under constant pressure to put out new works which were performed as soon as they were finished.
The Globe was an amphitheatre with several **galleries which held the seats**; if you were willing to pay extra money, you would be given a cushion. But the largest part of the audience, the groundlings or penny stinkers, would **stand in front and around the stage**. The theatres – much like football games or pop concerts nowadays – attracted **vast crowds** of people from all social ranks. This is something the playwrights had to consider when writing. In **Shakespeare**'s plays we can see how he **catered to different audiences**. We find coarse, cheesy and sentimental passages as well as philosophical, theological and witty ones.

His plays
His plays were and continue to be **extremely popular**. One of the reasons for this is **the themes** they deal with: They always regard **existential human experiences, feelings, fears and hopes**. No matter which milieu Shakespeare set his plays in (at court, in ancient Rome, in a fairytale world etc.), he always manages to reach out to his audience and make them identify with the characters or the situations, be it comedy or tragedy. Here is a **list**, which is in no way complete, of Shakespeare's major **themes** and some of the **plays** they are presented in:

- love vs. hate (Romeo and Juliet, Othello)
- injustice vs. justice (King Lear, Merchant of Venice)
- loyalty vs. betrayal (King Lear, Julius Caesar)
- deception vs. honesty (Othello, King Lear, Macbeth)
- ambition and crime (Othello, Macbeth)
- reflection and action (Hamlet, King Lear)
- disorder vs. God-given order (Macbeth, Hamlet)

His Language
Shakespeare wrote in an **early period of modern English** and very much left his own imprint on the language. The English language at the time was not yet as fixed with regard to grammar and spelling as it is today. The **Anglo-Saxon vocabulary** of Old English increased immensely due to **loanwords from Latin and French**. This meant that around 1600 there

were many synonyms for one and the same thing, e. g. playhouse – theatre; writer – poet; playgoers – audience etc. Thus, there was almost **no limit to creating new words** or playing with double meanings and creating rhymes, and Shakespeare took advantage of this fact.

His Poetry

Today we generally think of Shakespeare as being one of the world's greatest playwrights; yet, in his lifetime it may have been his poetry that he was most admired for, especially since poets had a better reputation than playwrights. His output was immense in this area as well, but he is certainly best known for his **sonnets**, of which he published **154**. The themes of the sonnets are: **mortality** of men and beauty, **immortality/transience** through art, the **joys and sorrows of love**.

Shakespeare developed his own poetic form by altering the well-known and often imitated Petrarchan rhyme scheme. **Shakespearean sonnets** consist of three **quatrains and one heroic or final couplet** resulting in a rhyme scheme of: abab cdcd efef gg.

His Fame

William Shakespeare is certainly regarded as the **most important English author** and even one of, if not the, **world's finest playwright**. His fame and popularity have lasted for over five centuries and one has observed something of a Shakespeare renaissance over the past two decades. While Shakespeare's **plays** have always been on **stages all over the world** (with numerous Asian and African companies discovering the plays and adopting them to their own unique non-European experiences), it has most recently been the moviemakers who have rediscovered the potential of Shakespeare's work. Screen adaptations like Kenneth Branagh's *Much Ado about Nothing*, Baz Luhrmann's *Romeo and Juliet* and of course the seven-time Oscar winning *Shakespeare in Love* were great box office successes, and the trend seems yet unbroken.

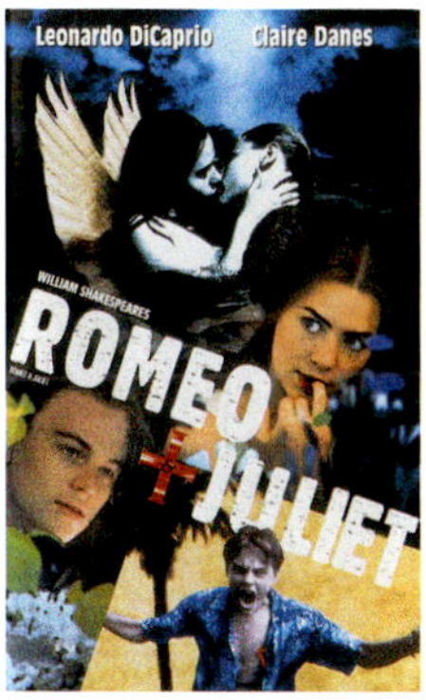

2. Wortschatz wiederholen und vertiefen – Elizabethan Age; Stylistic Devices

13 f.

1 Vocabulary in Context: His Age – The Elizabethan or the Golden Age

Fill in the correct words. The letters in bold type indicate the correct first letter.

Shakespeare wrote his works during the so-called **E**athliazben ________________[1] Age. The reign of Elizabeth I – with the defeat of the Spanish Armada in 1588 – marks the beginning of the **r**esi ________________[2] **of England to a world power** with **c**lnooies ________________[3] all over the globe. Therefore, it was a period of great **e**ococmin ________________[4], social and cultural change. But these changes were not exclusively due the altered political **b**aalcen ________________[5] in Europe, but also due to the occurrence of the **Rsnsneaiace** _______________[6]. It is commonly agreed that it began in Italy in the late 14th **c**netryu _______________[7] and **c**doinnuet _______________[8] in Western Europe through the 15th and 16th centuries; it did not reach England, however, until late in the 16th century. This period is often said to be the cradle of our modern times and the end of the **M**delid **A**sge _______________[9]. It derives its name from the **rediscovery** of the arts, philosophers and scholars of **a**ytiqntiu ____________[10], something which can be well observed when looking at some titles of Shakespeare's plays, like **Jsliuu Crsaea** _______________ _______________[11], Antony and **C**atrapoel ____________________[12], Titus Andronicus and Timon of Athens.

Nevertheless, Shakespeare's **c**ntreeomrpoais _______________[13] were still deeply rooted in their **m**deeivla _____________________[14] traditions and their Christian belief, which were carefully merged with the findings and ideas of Renaissance scholars. A concept which often provides a background for Shakespeare's dramas is the **Chain of B**ngei _________________[15]. It suggests that everything in the universe is organised in a **God-given hierarchy**. This hierarchical order in the (**m**rcoa ________________[16] -)**cosmos** is mirrored in the **m**rioc _________________[17]-**cosmos of men**. The social order is thus regarded as **G**vd-goien ______________[18] and may not be changed; if it is, this will lead to **c**oash ______________[19] within the micro-cosmos and will also be accompanied by chaos and unrest in the macro-cosmos. This can be seen, for example in Macbeth: The murder of the king leads to chaos in Scotland and also in nature; unnatural things keep occurring: "*Old Man: 'Tis unnatural, Even like the deed that's done. On Tuesday last A falcon, tow'ring in her pride of place, Was by a mousing owl hawked and killed.*" (Macbeth II, iv).

2 Analysing stylistic devices

ⓘ 29 f.

a. Read the examples taken from the works of William Shakespeare and identify which stylistic device they represent.

b. Fill the gaps in the *effects* column with the appropriate nouns/verbs/prepositions.

stylistic device	examples	possible effects/functions
____________	"Why then, O brawling love, O loving hate, O anything, of nothing first create!" *(Romeo and Juliet, I, i)*	to express a ____________ to show that sth. cannot be explained because it is b____________ reason
____________	"And yet, by heaven, I think my love as rare As any she belied with false compare." *(Sonnet 130)*	creation of surprise or suspense
____________	"Her traces, of the smallest spider web: Her collars, of the moonshine's watery beams; Her whip, of cricket's bone; the lash of film; Her wagoner, a small grey-coated gnat." *(Romeo and Juliet, I, iv)*	to put emphasis ____________ something
____________	"Whereat, with blade – with bloody, blameful blade – He bravely breached his boiling bloody breast." *(Midsummer Night's Dream, V, i)*	to produce a r____________ or in this case a c____________ effect
____________	"There's daggers in men's smiles" *(Macbeth, II, iii)*	to c____________ feelings that cannot be described, listener has to think twice; to offer new i____________ into the object of discussion
____________	"I'll have my bond! Speak not against my bond! I have sworn an oath that I will have my bond." *(Merchant of Venice, III, iii)*	to ____________ keywords; to em____________
____________	buzz, cuckoo, smack	v____________ illustration ____________ order to appeal ____________ the sense of hearing
____________	"My love is as a fever, longing still For that which longer nurseth the disease." *(Sonnet 147)*	to offer a new, often surprising insight ____________ the object of discussion
____________	"Life's but a walking shadow, a poor player That struts and frets his hour upon the stage, and then is heard no more." *(Macbeth, V, v)*	to depict something from a different p____________; to a____________ the readers' awareness; to open the readers' eyes to new experiences
____________	"What's a Montague? It is nor hand nor foot not any other part belonging to a man." *(Romeo and Juliet, II, ii)*	to emphasise; to raise t____________
____________	"This royal throne of kings, this scepter'd isle, This earth of majesty, this seat of Mars, This other Eden, demi-paradise, [...] Is now leased out – I die pronouncing it –" *(Richard II, II, i)*	to h____________ the effect; to s____________ a certain aspect; to ____________ sth. into the listener/ reader so the fact cannot be ignored

3. Eine Prüfungsaufgabe bearbeiten – Analyse eines Gedichts

28 f. 93 14; 15

William Shakespeare, Sonnet 18

Shall I compare thee to a summer's day?
Thou art more lovely and more temperate:
Rough winds do shake the darling buds of May,
And summer's lease hath all too short a date:

Sometime too hot the eye of heaven shines,
And often is his gold complexion dimm'd;
And every fair from fair sometime declines,
By chance or nature's changing course untrimm'd;

But thy eternal summer shall not fade
Nor lose possession of that fair thou owest;
Nor shall Death brag thou wander'st in his shade,
When in eternal lines to time thou growest:

So long as men can breathe or eyes can see,
So long lives this, and this gives life to thee.

3 Outline the content of the sonnet (Aufgabe 1: *comprehension*).

4 Analyse how the content of the sonnet is conveyed by the use of stylistic devices (Aufgabe 2: *analysis*).

If you need help, consult and complete the chart on the following page.

Sonnet 18	notes
Shall I compare thee to a summer's day? Thou art more lovely and more temperate: Rough winds do shake the darling buds of May, And summer's lease hath all too short a date:	*? ________________: to stress the contrast right away* *thou/thee/thy/more: r________________ to* *st________________ that the beloved person is different* *an________________: to st________________ the* *negative aspects of summer which are enum________________* *→ imperfection of summer*
Sometime too hot the eye of heaven shines, And often is his gold complexion dimm'd; And every fair from fair sometime declines, By chance or natures changing course untrimm'd;	? ________________: *effect?* *a*________________: unstoppable process of decline
But thy eternal summer shall not fade Nor lose possession of that fair thou owest; Nor shall Death brag thou wander'st in his shade, When in eternal lines to time thou growest:	r________________ of eternal *to* ________________ ? ________________: to point out the differences between beloved person and summer (*transience* ↔ e ________________) contrast is established: an________________ *nor* under-________________ the differences ? ________________: Grim Reaper (*Sensemann*); effect?
So long as men can breathe or eyes can see, So long lives this, and this gives life to thee.	an ________________ to s________________ that the poem will last forever → beloved person ________________

Aufgabenbeispiel 1:
Literarischer Text mit analytischem und produktionsorientiertem Schwerpunkt

Text: John Agard, *"Stereotype"* (in: John Agard, Limbo Dancer in Dark Glasses, Greenheart, London 1983)

John Agard: Stereotype

I'm a fullblooded
West Indian stereotype
See me straw hat?
Watch it good

I'm a fullblooded
West Indian stereotype
You ask
if I got riddum[1]
in me blood
You going ask!
Man just beat de drum
and don't forget
to pour de rum

I'm a fullblooded
West Indian stereotype
You say
I suppose you can show
us the limbo,[2] can't you?
How you know!
How you know!
You sure
you don't want me
sing you a calypso[3] too
How about that

I'm a fullblooded
West Indian stereotype
You call me
happy-go-lucky[4]
Yes that's me
dressing fancy
and chasing woman
if you think ah lie
bring yuh sister

I'm a fullblooded
West Indian stereotype
You wonder
where do you people
get such riddum

could it be the sunshine
My goodness
just listen to that steelband

Isn't there one thing
you forgot to ask
go on man ask ask
This native will answer anything
How about cricket?[5]
suppose you're good at it?
Hear this man
good at it!
Put de willow[6]
in me hand
and watch me strike
de boundary[7]

Yes I'm a fullblooded
West Indian stereotype

that's why I
graduated from Oxford University
with a degree
in anthropology[8]

---

[1]**riddum**: rhythm – [2]**limbo**: Caribbean dance in which the dancer bends back and passes under a bar that is gradually lowered – [3]**calypso**: music style that is popular throughout the Caribbean (played by steelbands) – [4]**happy-go-lucky**: (adj.) carefree – [5]**cricket**: the West Indian cricket team is among the best in the world – [6]**willow**: *here*: cricket bat – [7]**strike de boundary**: (in cricket) way of getting the most points – [8]**anthropology**: study of mankind

Assignments:

1. Outline what is characteristic of a "fullblooded West Indian stereotype" (l. 1 f.) according to the poem (*comprehension*).

2. Analyse how the poet conveys the speaker's attitudes and feelings (*analysis*).

3. Turn this poem into a speech given by a West Indian student of anthropology in Oxford (*evaluation: re-creation of text*).

Aufgabenbeispiel 2:
Sachtext mit analytisch-interpretierendem Schwerpunkt

Text: Jeffrey Sachs, "Climate sceptics are recycled critics of controls on tobacco and acid rain" (in: The Guardian; 19 February 2010)

We must not be distracted from science's urgent message: we are fuelling dangerous changes in Earth's climate

In the weeks before and after the Copenhagen climate change Conference last December, the science of climate change came under harsh attack by critics who contend that climate scientists have deliberately suppressed evidence – and that the science itself is severely flawed. The Intergovernmental Panel on Climate Change (IPCC), the global group of experts charged with assessing the state of climate science, has been accused of bias.
The global public is disconcerted by these attacks. If experts cannot agree that there is a climate crisis, why should governments spend billions of dollars to address it?
The fact is that the critics – who are few in number but aggressive in their attacks – are deploying tactics that they have honed for more than 25 years. During their long campaign, they have greatly exaggerated scientific disagreements in order to stop action on climate change, with special interests like Exxon Mobil footing the bill.
Many books have recently documented the games played by the climate-change deniers. Merchants of Doubt, a new book by Naomi Oreskes and Erik Conway set for release in mid-2010, will be an authoritative account of their misbehaviour. The authors show that the same group of mischief-makers, given a platform by the free-market ideologues of *The Wall Street* Journal's editorial page, has consistently tried to confuse the public and discredit the scientists whose insights are helping to save the world from unintended environmental harm. Today's campaigners against action on climate change are in many cases backed by the same lobbies, individuals, and organisations that sided with the tobacco industry to discredit the science linking smoking and lung cancer. Later, they fought the scientific evidence that sulphur oxides from coal-fired power plants were causing "acid rain." Then, when it was discovered that certain chemicals called chlorofluorocarbons (CFCs) were causing the depletion of ozone in the atmosphere, the same groups launched a nasty campaign to discredit that science, too. [...]
What is amazing is that, although these attacks on science have been wrong for 30 years, they still sow doubts about established facts. The truth is that there is big money backing the climate-change deniers, whether it is companies that don't want to pay the extra costs of regulation, or free-market ideologues opposed to any government controls.
The latest round of attacks involves two episodes. The first was the hacking of a climate-change research centre in England. The emails that were stolen suggested a lack of forthrightness in the presentation of some climate data. Whatever the details of this specific case, the studies in question represent a tiny fraction of the overwhelming scientific evidence that points to the reality and urgency of man-made climate change.
The second issue was a blatant error concerning glaciers that appeared in a major IPCC report. Here it should be understood that the IPCC issues thousands of pages of text. There are, no doubt, errors in those pages. But errors in the midst of a vast and complex report

by the IPCC point to the inevitability of human shortcomings, not to any fundamental flaws in climate science.

When the emails and the IPCC error were brought to light, editorial writers at *The Wall Street Journal* launched a vicious campaign describing climate science as a hoax and a conspiracy. They claimed that scientists were fabricating evidence in order to obtain government research grants – a ludicrous accusation, [...] Climate change science is a wondrous intellectual activity. Great scientific minds have learned over the course of many decades to "read" the Earth's history, in order to understand how the climate system works. [...]

The IPCC and the climate scientists are telling us a crucial message. We need urgently to transform our energy, transport, food, industrial, and construction Systems to reduce the dangerous human impact on the climate. It is our responsibility to listen, to understand the message, and then to act.

Assignments:

1. Outline what the articie reports on the latest discoveries of scientific flaws in the UN climate report (Fourth Assessment Report, AR4) from 2007 published by the IPCC, and what consequences the author demands. *(comprehension)*
2. Analyse how the author tries to convince the reader of his opinions. *(analysis)*
3. Write a letter to the editor to *The Guardian* explaining why you disagree with the article. You should refer to content and style. *(evaluation: re-creation of text)*

Umgang mit den Checklisten

1. Kurzinfo: schneller Überblick über die wichtigsten Kennzeichen bestimmter Textsorten
2. Selbstevaluation: überprüfen, ob bei der Bearbeitung einer Aufgabe alle wichtigen Aspekte beachtet wurden und Text gegebenenfalls überarbeiten

Checkliste – Textzusammenfassung

16 f. | 53 f. | 4 f.; 14

	wichtige Aspekte	beachtet	nicht beachtet
Inhalt	**einleitender Satz** – Titel, Verfasser, Publikationsdatum, Thema –		
	Zusammenfassung **relevanter** Informationen (Operator!)		
kommunikative Textgestaltung	Struktur: erkennbar strukturierte einzelne Abschnitte (*topic sentence!*)		
	logische Verknüpfung der einzelnen Gedanken (*connectives!*)		
	Beachtung der Normen der Textsorte: keine Textverweise		
	Beachtung der Normen der Textsorte: Grundtempus Simple Present		
Ausdrucksvermögen	Loslösung von Formulierungen des Ausgangstextes (eigene Worte)		
	Verwendung der *useful phrases*		
Sprachrichtigkeit	Rechtschreibung		
	Grammatik		
	präzise Wortwahl		

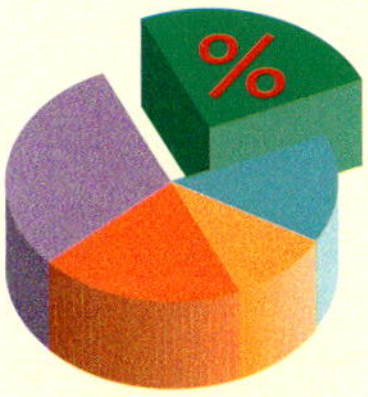

Checkliste – Analyse von Statistiken

ⓘ 17 f.

	wichtige Aspekte	beachtet	nicht beachtet
Inhalt	**Einleitung** – Quelle/Fundstelle/Publikationsjahr; Art der Darstellung (pie/bar chart; table; line graph); Thema; behandelter Zeitraum –		
	Beschreibung der Statistik		
	Interpretation der Statistik – Entwicklungen; Höhepunkte; Beziehungen zwischen Daten –		
	zusammenfassende **Schlussfolgerung** (evtl. Einbeziehung von Hintergrundwissen) und **Bewertung** (manipulativ? verlässlich? aktuell? einseitig?)		
kommunikative Textgestaltung	Struktur: erkennbare Gliederung des Textes		
	Struktur: erkennbar strukturierte einzelne Abschnitte (*topic sentence*!)		
	logische Verknüpfung der einzelnen Gedanken (*connectives*!)		
	Beachtung der Normen der Textsorte: Grundtempus Simple Present		
Ausdrucksvermögen	Verwendung der *useful phrases*		
Sprachrichtigkeit	Rechtschreibung		
	Grammatik		
	präzise Wortwahl		

Checkliste – Analyse von Karikaturen

19 f. 74 f. 11

	wichtige Aspekte	beachtet	nicht beachtet
Inhalt	**Einleitung** – Thema; Karikaturist; Publikationsort/-datum –		
	detaillierte **Beschreibung** von Bild und Text		
	Analyse/Interpretation – Bezug zu (aktuellen) politischen oder geschichtlichen Ereignissen/Persönlichkeiten; Interpretation von Symbolen/Anspielungen; Analyse der Darstellung der Personen und deren Beziehungen		
	zusammenfassende **Schlussfolgerung** – Wirkung; Intention –		
kommunikative Textgestaltung	<u>Struktur</u>: erkennbare Gliederung		
	<u>Struktur</u>: erkennbar strukturierte einzelne Abschnitte (*topic sentence*!)		
	logische Verknüpfung der einzelnen Gedanken (*connectives*!)		
	<u>Beachtung der Normen der Textsorte:</u> Grundtempus Simple Present		
Ausdrucksvermögen	Verwendung von *useful phrases*		
Sprachrichtigkeit	Rechtschreibung		
	Grammatik		
	präzise Wortwahl		

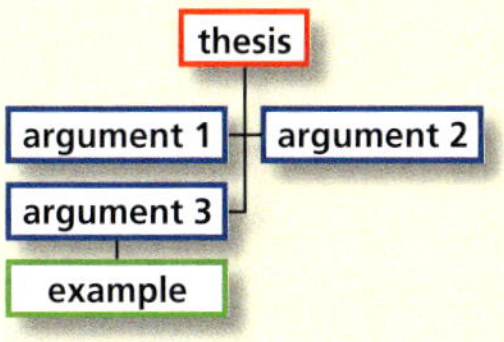

Checkliste – Analyse der Argumentationsstruktur (*composition*)

21 f. 44 f. 1 f.

	wichtige Aspekte	beachtet	nicht beachtet
Inhalt	**einleitender Satz**		
	Analyse der **Einleitung** – Wie wird Aufmerksamkeit geweckt? (Beispiele? These?) –		
	Analyse der **Struktur** des Textes – These, Argumente, Beispiele etc. –		
	Gegenüberstellungen oder Vergleiche von Argumenten/Thesen/Ideen?		
	wiederkehrende **Themen/Motive**?		
	Überzeugung durch **Qualität oder Quantität der Argumente?**		
	Analyse des **Fazits** – Bezug zur Einleitung?; Ausblick? –		
	Zusammenfassung		
kommunikative Textgestaltung	Struktur: erkennbare Gliederung		
	Struktur: erkennbar strukturierte einzelne Abschnitte (*topic sentence*!)		
	logische Verknüpfung der einzelnen Gedanken (*connectives*!)		
	Beachtung der Normen der Textsorte: Grundtempus Simple Present		
	angemessene Textverweise/Zitate		
Ausdrucksvermögen	Verwendung der *useful phrases*		
Sprachrichtigkeit	Rechtschreibung		
	Grammatik		
	präzise Wortwahl		

Checkliste – Analyse rhetorischer Mittel

22 f. 48 f. 3 f.; 11

	wichtige Aspekte	beachtet	nicht beachtet
Inhalt	**einleitender Satz**		
	z. B. **Hervorhebung** bestimmter Aspekte – *repetition; anaphora; alliteration* –		
	z. B. **Einbeziehung** der Leser – bzw. Zuhörerschaft – *use of first person plural pronoun; direct address; rhetorical question* –		
	z. B. **Illustrieren und Emotionen wecken** – *vivid descriptions; personifications; similes; metaphors; enumerations of examples; gradations; irony/sarcasm; hyperboles* –		
	z. B. (scheinbar) **sachliche Absicherung der Argumente** des Autors/Sprechers – *quoting experts/statistics; claims; enumerations of examples* –		
	Zusammenfassung		
kommunikative Textgestaltung	<u>Struktur</u>: erkennbare Gliederung gemäß der verschiedenen Funktionen der rhetorischen Mittel		
	<u>Struktur</u>: erkennbar strukturierte einzelne Abschnitte (*topic sentence*!)		
	logische Verknüpfung der einzelnen Gedanken (*connectives*!)		
	<u>Beachtung der Normen der Textsorte:</u> Grundtempus Simple Present		
	angemessene Textverweise/Zitate		
Ausdrucksvermögen	Verwendung der *useful phrases*		
Sprachrichtigkeit	Rechtschreibung		
	Grammatik		
	präzise Wortwahl		

Checkliste – Schreiben eines argumentativen Textes

ⓘ 25 f.

	wichtige Aspekte	beachtet	nicht beachtet
Inhalt	**Einleitung** – Beispiel; Zitat; rhetorische Fragen; Fakten; ironische Bemerkungen … –		
	Darlegung der **eigenen Meinung**		
	(Darlegung **möglicher Gegenargumente**)		
	Darlegung der **Argumente für die eigene Meinung**		
	Untermauerung der Argumente durch **Beispiele**		
	Zusammenfassung		
kommunikative Textgestaltung	<u>Struktur</u>: erkennbare Gliederung		
	<u>Struktur</u>: erkennbar strukturierte einzelne Abschnitte pro Argument (*topic sentence; explanation; examples*)		
	logische Verknüpfung der einzelnen Gedanken (*connectives*?)		
	evtl. Verwendung rhetorischer Mittel		
	<u>Beachtung der Normen der Textsorte:</u> Grundtempus Simple Present		
Ausdrucksvermögen	Verwendung der *useful phrases*		
Sprachrichtigkeit	Rechtschreibung		
	Grammatik		
	präzise Wortwahl		

Checkliste – Verfassen eines Leserbriefs

27 74 f. 12

	wichtige Aspekte	beachtet	nicht beachtet
Inhalt	**einleitender Satz** – Bezug zu Artikel; Autor; Zeitungsausgabe –		
	begründete Darlegung der eigenen Meinung		
kommunikative Textgestaltung	<u>Struktur</u>: erkennbare Gliederung		
	<u>Struktur</u>: erkennbar strukturierte einzelne Abschnitte pro Argument (*topic sentence; explanation; examples*)		
	logische Verknüpfung der einzelnen Gedanken (*connectives*!)		
	evtl. Verwendung rhetorischer Mittel		
Normen der Textsorte	Absender; ohne Namen!		
	Empfängeradresse		
	Datum		
	Anrede (ohne *Dear*!)		
	Briefende (Name, Ort)		
	Grundtempus Simple Present		
Ausdrucksvermögen	Verwendung der *useful phrases*		
Sprachrichtigkeit	Rechtschreibung		
	Grammatik		
	präzise Wortwahl		

Checkliste – Gedichtanalyse

29 f. 80 f. 15

	wichtige Aspekte	beachtet	nicht beachtet
Inhalt	**einleitender Satz**		
	Aufbau des Gedichts – *stanzas; lines; rhyme scheme* –		
	Atmosphäre/Stimmung?		
	Wortwahl: viele Verben → aktiv; Beschreibung einer Handlung; viele Adjektive → passiv; Zustandsbeschreibung		
	Benennung von Stilmitteln und deren Wirkung in Bezug auf das Thema des Gedichts		
	Zusammenfassung		
kommunikative Textgestaltung	Struktur: erkennbare Gliederung		
	Struktur: erkennbar strukturierte einzelne Abschnitte (*topic sentence*!)		
	logische Verknüpfung der einzelnen Gedanken (*connectives*!)		
	Beachtung der Normen der Textsorte: Grundtempus Simple Present		
	angemessene Textverweise/Zitate		
Ausdrucksvermögen	Verwendung der *useful phrases*		
Sprachrichtigkeit	Rechtschreibung		
	Grammatik		
	präzise Wortwahl		

Checkliste – Analyse des *settings*

31 f. 58 f. 5

	wichtige Aspekte	beachtet	nicht beachtet
Inhalt	**einleitender Satz**		
	Grundinformationen zu **Ort und Zeit**		
	Atmosphäre – Wetter; Jahreszeit; Tageszeit; Beschreibung des Ortes; Symbole … –		
	Widerspiegelung bzw. Kontrastierung der Gefühle der literarischen Figuren durch die Beschreibung von Ort und Zeit		
	Einleitung bzw. Illustrierung des Themas		
	Zusammenfassung		
kommunikative Textgestaltung	Struktur: erkennbare Gliederung		
	Struktur: erkennbar strukturierte einzelne Abschnitte (*topic sentence*!)		
	logische Verknüpfung der einzelnen Gedanken (*connectives*!)		
	Beachtung der Normen der Textsorte: Grundtempus Simple Present		
	angemessene Textverweise/Zitate		
Ausdrucksvermögen	Verwendung der *useful phrases*		
Sprachrichtigkeit	Rechtschreibung		
	Grammatik		
	präzise Wortwahl		

Checkliste – Analyse der Erzählperspektive

32 f. 70 f. 9

	wichtige Aspekte	beachtet	nicht beachtet
Inhalt	**einleitender Satz** – Bezug zur Fragestellung herstellen –		
	first-person point of view? – first- person narrator? – stream of consciousness? **third-person point of view**? – third-person limited point of view? – omniscient narrator?		
	Beschreibung der **Wirkungen der Erzählperspektive** im Hinblick auf den Schwerpunkt der **Aufgabenstellung**		
	Zusammenfassung		
kommunikative Textgestaltung	Struktur: erkennbare Gliederung		
	Struktur: erkennbar strukturierte einzelne Abschnitte (*topic sentence*!)		
	logische Verknüpfung der einzelnen Gedanken (*connectives*!)		
	Beachtung der Normen der Textsorte: Grundtempus Simple Present		
	angemessene Textverweise/Zitate		
Ausdrucksvermögen	Verwendung der *useful phrases*		
Sprachrichtigkeit	Rechtschreibung		
	Grammatik		
	präzise Wortwahl		

Checkliste – Charakterisierung

34 f. 62 f. 7 f.

	wichtige Aspekte	beachtet	nicht beachtet
Inhalt	**einleitender Satz**		
	Eckdaten – Alter; Beruf; Familie … –		
	äußeres **Erscheinungsbild**		
	Haltungen/Wünsche/allgemeine Charakter-eigenschaften		
	Verhalten in im Text(auszug) beschriebenen **Situationen**		
	Verhalten/Gefühle gegenüber **anderen** literarischen Figuren		
	persönliche Entwicklung (Krisen; Wendepunkte)		
	Zusammenfassung		
kommunikative Textgestaltung	Struktur: erkennbare Gliederung		
	Struktur: erkennbar strukturierte einzelne Abschnitte (*topic sentence*!)		
	logische Verknüpfung der einzelnen Gedanken (*connectives*!)		
	Beachtung der Normen der Textsorte: Grundtempus Simple Present		
	angemessene Textverweise/Zitate		
Ausdrucksvermögen	Verwendung der *useful phrases*		
Sprachrichtigkeit	Rechtschreibung		
	Grammatik		
	präzise Wortwahl		

Checkliste – Kreativer Schreibauftrag

35 f. | 67; 70 f. | 8; 9

	wichtige Aspekte	beachtet	nicht beachtet
Inhalt	**keine Widersprüche** zum Ausgangstext		
	wesentliche Details des Ausgangstextes werden erwähnt		
	geforderte Perspektive wurde eingehalten – wird deutlich in: Sprache; Stil; (un)eingeschränkter Wahrnehmung; Haltungen; Eigenschaften … –		
	inhaltlicher Schwerpunkt entspricht der Aufgabenstellung		
kommunikative Textgestaltung	Beachtung der **Normen der Textsorte** (Kennzeichen von formalen und informellen Briefen; Tagebucheintrag …)		
	Sprache entspricht der **Textsorte**		
Ausdrucksvermögen	**Sprache** entspricht den **Adressaten**		
	Sprache entspricht der **Situation**		
Sprachrichtigkeit	Rechtschreibung		
	Grammatik		
	präzise Wortwahl		

Checkliste – Deutung von Regie-anweisungen

ⓘ 36 f.

	wichtige Aspekte	beachtet	nicht beachtet
Inhalt	**einleitender Satz** – Bezug zur Fragestellung herstellen –		
	Grundinformationen – Aussehen; Alter; Beruf; Ort; Zeit –		
	Informationen zum **räumlichen Abstand** zu anderen Figuren und deren **Deutung**		
	Informationen zur **Gestik und Mimik** und deren **Deutung**		
	Informationen zu **Handlungen** und deren **Deutung**		
	Informationen zu **Gefühlen** und deren **Deutung**		
	Zusammenfassung		
kommunikative Textgestaltung	Struktur: erkennbare Gliederung		
	Struktur: erkennbar strukturierte einzelne Abschnitte (*topic sentence*!)		
	logische Verknüpfung der einzelnen Gedanken (*connectives*!)		
	Beachtung der Normen der Textsorte: Grundtempus Simple Present		
	angemessene Textverweise/Zitate		
Ausdrucksvermögen	Verwendung von *useful phrases*		
Sprachrichtigkeit	Rechtschreibung		
	Grammatik		
	präzise Wortwahl		

Checkliste – Analyse von *stills*

39 f. 70 f. 9

	wichtige Aspekte	beachtet	nicht beachtet
Inhalt	**einleitender Satz** – Bezug zur Fragestellung herstellen (evtl.: Kontextualisierung des *stills*; Thesen des Textes zu *still* in Beziehung setzen) –		
	Beschreibung des *stills*		
	(Beschreibung der **Atmosphäre**)		
	Bestimmung des ***camera range*** und dessen **Deutung**		
	Bestimmung des ***camera angles*** und dessen **Deutung**		
	Bestimmung der ***camera position*** und deren **Deutung**		
	Zusammenfassung		
kommunikative Textgestaltung	<u>Struktur</u>: erkennbare Gliederung		
	<u>Struktur</u>: erkennbar strukturierte einzelne Abschnitte (*topic sentence*!)		
	logische Verknüpfung der einzelnen Gedanken (*connectives*!)		
	<u>Beachtung der Normen der Textsorte:</u> Grundtempus Simple Present		
	(Rückbezug zum Text)		
Ausdrucksvermögen	Verwendung von *useful phrases*		
Sprachrichtigkeit	Rechtschreibung		
	Grammatik		
	präzise Wortwahl		

Bildnachweis

S. 20: © www.KUNSTSAM.de; S. 28, 29, 34 (6 Illustrationen), 42 o., 47 u., 50, 60, 76 l., 88, 90, 91, 93, 94, 95, 96: Reinhild Kassing/Verlagsarchiv Schöningh; S. 39 (4 Bilder), 41 (3 Bilder): © 1999 Dreamworks L.L.C.; S. 40 (6 Bilder): © 2002 Iconolatry Productions Inc.; S. 42 u.: UN Photo / Eskinder Debebe; S. 43: UN; S. 46 u.: © dpa-Fotoreport; S. 47 o.: Jose Giribas; S. 51: taken from: http://weblog.chrisgrundemann.com/index.php/2009/become-cyborg-free/; S. 56 o.: Andy Wear; S. 56 u.: taken from: http://www.paradise-engineering.com/utopia/index.html; S. 57: vwork; S. 61 o.: mediacolors; S. 61 u.: ullstein bild - Granger Collection; S. 64 r.u.: Bildarchiv Preußischer Kulturbesitz (bpk), Berlin; S. 64 l.o.: John Hill; S. 64 r.o.: Philippe-Jaques de Loutherbourg; S. 65 r.o.: Punch, 1892; S. 65 r.u.: picture-alliance / KPA/TopFoto; S. 69 o.: Foto: Michael Hughes/ZENIT; S. 69 u.l.: Monica Ali, Brick Lane, Scribner, 2008 (cover); S. 69 u.r.: Zadie Smith, White Teeth, Penguin, 2002 (cover); S. 71: Distributed by Optimum Releasing Ltd. Artwork © 2008 Optimum Releasing Ltd.; S. 75: taken from: http://markjones4mp.blogspot.com/2008_12_01_archive.html; S. 76 r.: picture-alliance / dpa; S. 77: CINETEXT Bildarchiv, Frankfurt; weitere: Verlagsarchiv Schöningh

Sollte trotz aller Bemühungen um korrekte Urheberangaben ein Irrtum unterlaufen sein, bitten wir darum, sich mit dem Verlag in Verbindung zu setzen, damit wir eventuell erforderliche Korrekturen vornehmen können.